ONE BEST HIKE

YOSEMITE'S HALF DOME

ONE BEST HIKE

YOSEMITE'S HALF DOME

Everything you need to know to successfully hike Yosemite's most famous landmark

Rick Deutsch

 WILDERNESS PRESS ... *on the trail since 1967*

BERKELEY, CA

One Best Hike: Yosemite's Half Dome

1st EDITION May 2007
  2nd printing May 2008
  3rd printing June 2009

Copyright © 2007 by Rick Deutsch

Cover photo credits:
Top front and top back copyright © 2007 by Mathew Grimm
Middle front copyright © 2007 by Rick Deutsch
Bottom front and bottom back copyright © 2007 by Michael McKay

Interior photos, except where noted, by Rick Deutsch
Frontispiece photo by Mathew Grimm
Vintage photos on pages 10, 26, 89, 92 courtesy Yosemite Museum, National Park
  Service

Cover design: Larry B. Van Dyke
Book design and layout: Andreas Schueller

ISBN 978-0-89997-443-9

Manufactured in Canada

Published by: **Wilderness Press**
                  1345 8th Street
                  Berkeley, CA 94710
                  (800) 443-7227; FAX (510) 558-1696
                  info@wildernesspress.com
                  www.wildernesspress.com

Visit our website for a complete listing of our books and for ordering information.

Front cover photos: Top: Half Dome from a distance; *Middle:* The cables up Half
  Dome; *Bottom:* Overhang on the summit of Half Dome
Back cover photos: Top: Half Dome from Four Mile Trail; *Bottom:* The cable route up
  Half Dome
Frontispiece: View of Half Dome

Acknowledgments

I would like to thank:

My wife Diane for her patience during my many hikes of Half Dome and the hours I spent at the keyboard; my sister, Michelle LaMarche, who did the hike several times before I did and encouraged me to do it the first time; the Yosemite Association for its support of this precious American resource and for the fine articles in its publications; the Decathlon Club in Santa Clara, California, where I spend endless hours in training; my friends and family, who have done the hike with me and inspired me to write this book.

Carpe diem. Seize the day.

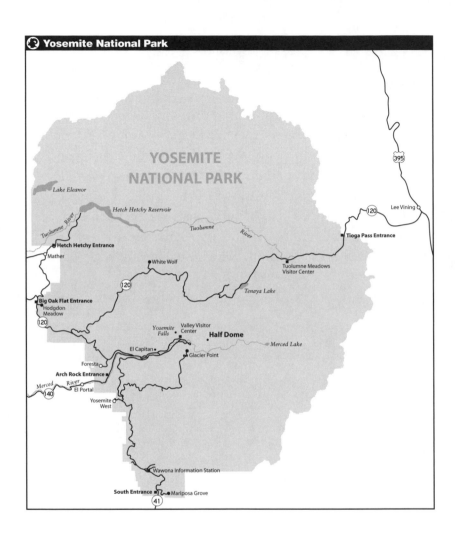

Contents

Preface

The motto for my life is "Carpe Diem." This is a Latin phrase meaning "Seize the Day." It is believed to have originated with the ancient philosopher, Horace, the leading Roman lyric poet during the time of Augustus Caesar. Another interpretation would be: "Smell the rose today, for it may be wilted tomorrow."

My first Half Dome hike, in 1990, transformed me from an "I'll-do-XYZ-someday" person to someone booking reservations for adventure trips *now*. We all have a finite number of heartbearts allocated to us and one day, "tomorrow" will not come. Get out and live life. Experience things while you can. Hike Half Dome. Too many of my friends have become unable to live their dreams due to injuries, illness, finances, age, or family issues.

Try this exercise. Write down all the things you want to do or see or experience before you die. Now write down the number of years you think you will remain ambulatory and able physically and mentally to attempt those things. Next, consider how much free time you will have available. This should be your private list—only put down the things that you personally want to do. Whether you get two, three, or four weeks of vacation, remember that you'll likely use some of that time for weddings, funerals, and family events. A few of your major "wants" may take two weeks or more (a safari, a trip to the South Pole, a bike ride across America). You will see that there is not enough time left to do the whole list—let alone repeat the more spectacular entries on it.

Put down the TV remote and strap on your hiking boots, or ride your bike, or swim, or run, or just smell that rose today.

Rick Deutsch
San Jose, CA
April 2007

✿ *1* ✿
Introduction

No Temple made with hands can compare with Yosemite. Every rock in its walls seems to glow with life; the true ownership of the wilderness belongs in the highest degree to those who love it most.

— John Muir

"Yosemite"—the very name evokes images of verdant valleys, cascading waterfalls, peaceful meadows, soaring mountains, arching domes, meandering rivers, lush forests, diverse wildlife, and 2000-year-old giant sequoias. These 1200 square miles, located in California's Sierra Nevada mountain range, are the crown jewel of the National Park Service. Yosemite has become a "must-see" on the list of every outdoor enthusiast. The park's natural wonders attract people of all kinds, be they old, young, citizens, or foreigners. With this popularity comes the crush of humanity—out to explore the wonders of nature, many sporting only a daypack, a bottle of water, and a desire to see this wild environment as it has existed for centuries. Yosemite's hikes are superb, from short jaunts of a couple of hours duration to expeditions of several days. The Yosemite Valley comprises only 1 percent

Yosemite's Half Dome

of the park but is one of the most popular destinations in the National Park system. Ninety-five percent of Yosemite is designated Wilderness.

The Yosemite General Management Plan, drawn up in 1980, cites as one of its goals the promotion of visitor understanding and enjoyment. This is in direct support of the stated purpose set forth in 1864 when Yosemite was designated an inalienable public trust (it became a national park in 1890): to make its resources available to people for their enjoyment, education, and recreation, now and in the future.

In a great honor, Yosemite was selected as the theme for California on the 2005 U.S. quarter coin. California's quarter depicts naturalist and conservationist John Muir admiring Yosemite's monolithic granite headwall known as Half Dome. It bears the inscriptions "California," "John Muir," "Yosemite Valley," and "1850," the year the state was admitted into the Union. When you consider the varied attractions of California, it is indeed a testament to have Yosemite (and Half Dome) represent the Golden State to the country and the world. Yosemite has been recognized internationally as well: in 1984 it was designated a World Heritage Site by the UN.

One of the favorite day trips in Yosemite is up to the top of Half Dome, at the eastern edge of Yosemite Valley. This is an impressive hike—a full 10- to 12-hour day for most people, comprising nearly 16 miles round trip. Included is a dramatic 425-foot vertical climb up the nearly 45-degree incline of Half Dome's granite slope. Not to worry; this is accomplished with the aid of two steel cable handrails.

This guide is for those in reasonable condition. If you've maintained an adequate fitness level and consider yourself in good shape and are not afraid of sweating, then you should have no trouble completing the Half Dome hike.

This guide is for those in reasonable condition. If you've maintained an adequate fitness level and consider yourself in good shape and are not afraid of sweating, then you should have no trouble completing the Half Dome hike.

This book is also aimed at those who have a genuine interest in learning about the history of the park, the lives of the Native Americans, and the roles of early explorers and modern conservationists. The focus is on Half Dome. It's for the person who has thought about doing the hike but doesn't know much about it. Preparation, conditioning, and planning are all prerequisites. Your adventure will involve strength, stamina, and discovery, and this guide will prepare you to be self-reliant.

The hike can be done in one day, or more leisurely in two days if you want to backpack. This guidebook describes the most popular route to the summit. Regardless of your strategy, it will help you prepare prior to leaving home and then help steer you up the mountain on your summit day. My intent is to provide a resource that can enable nearly anyone physically able to complete the hike. Further, I believe that this educational guide will enhance visitor understanding and enjoyment of park resources.

I first hiked Half Dome in 1990 and was so moved by the experience that I decided to do it annually. As of press time, I've done the hike 19 times. My motivation goes back to the sixth-century tale of Milo of Kroton (a Greek colony in a southern Italy). It seems that, as a boy, Milo would pick up a small calf on a daily basis. As the calf grew larger, Milo continued to lift the animal, and the boy became stronger. His muscles became so powerful that he could carry the animal with ease when it became a full-sized ox. This constant yet gradual training resulted in Milo developing into a man of incredible strength, so much so that he won the ancient Olympic wrestling title a remarkable six consecutive times. He was likely an actual historical person as he is mentioned by many classical authors, among them Aristotle. Okay, perhaps this is a poor analogy, but maybe by working out on a regular basis and staying in condition for this hike, I hope to live a few years longer than the actuarial tables project.

While on these hikes, I have noticed many unprepared optimists setting out, knowing little of what lay ahead. Their poor preparation was obvious. I have seen many people suffer from a lack of water, sore muscles, inferior shoes, and a big underestimation of the magnitude of the hike. And yet, I've found no other Half Dome-specific hiking guides. There are many general "Hiking-in-Yosemite" books, but they cover Half Dome in only a few pages. This guide should fill your knowledge gaps and allow you to hit the trail with confidence.

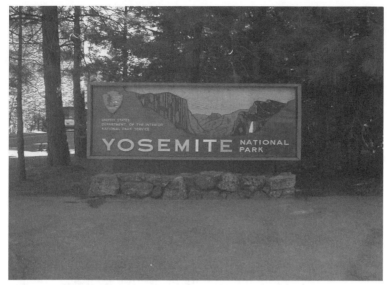

Welcome to Yosemite!

This book was designed to be small and fit into your pack, so take it on your hike. There will be many people on the trail—you won't get lost. I've included photos of much of the trail, so you won't wonder what's in store. Although these pictures show the high points of the hike, nothing will replace your seeing these majestic sights yourself. Finally, all opinions and suggestions are mine. Others may approach these topics differently or disagree with me. Pick out what you like and make informed decisions.

The History of Yosemite and Half Dome

Volumes have been written on the geological and human history of Yosemite, so I'll defer to other sources for a detailed account. The area's origins can be traced back some 500 million years to when the entire region was an ancient seabed. Deep below the ground, constant earth movement and the effects of pressure and heat created magma. This molten rock far beneath the surface rose and cooled into a massive granite hulk that extended 80 by 400 miles and became the core of the Sierra Nevada. (The mountains are still rising today, at a rate of 1 foot every 1000 years.)

The eroding action of river flows and glacial activity eventually carved Yosemite Valley into its present shape. Over time, rivers cut distinct paths and erosion shaped the landscape. Later, glaciers settled in, and thus began the slow battle between ice and stone. Many of Yosemite's tall domes were actually above the glaciers, but constant cycles of freezing and thawing led to "exfoliation," that is, large sheets of granite flaking off in vertical patterns. In time, the valley was left with a fertile bed of rich soil.

Yosemite is undergoing change even now. Occasional fires ravage parts of the park. Rockslides as recently as 1996 and 1999 dropped enormous sheets of granite near Happy Isles. They produced massive shock waves that snapped thousands of trees. Events like these are unpredictable, and are a reminder that Yosemite is undergoing constant change. The Merced River flood of 1997 set records, and the high watermarks are still visible. A huge rockslide just outside the park on Hwy. 140 closed that road for part of 2006. These phenomena are reminders of Yosemite's dynamic state.

Half Dome is estimated to be nearly 90 million years old. It is the signature monument of Yosemite and is truly an American and a world icon. It is the one of the planet's most vertical walls, with the northwest face rising 2000 feet nearly straight up. Its peak reaches an altitude of 8842 feet. The distinctive face reflects earth's primordial power. It is not a true spherical dome; when viewed from the west, it appears as a rounded table rather than the "half-football" image it presents from other angles. It's estimated that only 20 percent of the original dome is gone. With an altitude gain of 4737

Aerial view of the backside of Half Dome

Marty Gerbasi

feet above the valley floor, a hiker will ascend almost a mile vertically!

The earliest Native Americans arrived in this area about 1000 BC. Today, we know their descendants as the "Ahwahneechee," from the Miwok Indian name for the valley, Ahwahnee, or "place of a gaping mouth." They called Half Dome "Tis-sa-ack," meaning "Cleft Rock," in honor of a maiden whose teary profile is believed to be captured on its face for all time. The spelling of these Miwok words is a guess, as the tribe had no written language.

The first explorer to see the park was Joseph Walker, in 1833. He was hunting beaver in the Sierra and passed by the Yosemite area as he continued to Monterey. The great California Gold Rush started in 1848, just 100 miles to the north. However, Yosemite wasn't entered by non-Indians until 1851. At that time the Mariposa Battalion, organized to quell hostilities between the Indians and local miners and settlers, pursued the Indians into their Yosemite Valley home. This first formal contact was documented by the Battalion doctor, Lafayette H. Bunnell, in his 1880 book on the discovery of Yosemite. The early meetings with the leader of the Ahwaneechee Chief Ten-ie-ya (Tenaya) provided a wealth of knowledge about the valley. When Chief Ten-ie-ya died in 1853, the remaining Yosemite Indians dispersed and Yosemite Valley became a white man's settlement. In 1854 the first organized commercial tours of Yosemite Valley began. The next year, James Hutchings led a tour party, and he kindled interest through his writings in his San Francisco illustrated work, *Hutchings' Illustrated California Magazine.* He later authored many popular books on Yosemite. The lands of Yosemite were charted in 1863 by the U.S. Geologic Survey of California. Early visitors originally called Half Dome "South Dome," because they felt it balanced "North Dome" across the valley. However, the current name, Half Dome, was soon the common name.

John Muir's writings influenced the country so much that, in 1890, Yosemite obtained federal protection as a national park.

To help protect the pristine environs from commercial interests, in June 1864 President Abraham Lincoln signed the Yosemite Grant, which deeded Yosemite Valley and the Mariposa Grove of Big Trees (at the southern end) to the state of California. The bill mandated that this land be used for resort and recreation, "for all time." Galen Clark was the first caretaker of the park. John Muir arrived in 1868, and his writings influenced the country so much that, in 1890, Yosemite obtained federal protection as a national park. Today the park has two guardians: the National Park Service and the nonprofit Yosemite Association, which work to preserve and protect the park for future generations.

The First Ascent of Half Dome

Climbing up Half Dome was considered impossible until October 1875, when George Anderson, a Scottish blacksmith and jack-of-all-trades, labored weeks to drill holes into the granite of the backside to create a ropeway made up of a five-strand, 975-foot-long rope. The knotted rope was affixed through eyelets that Anderson put into the holes he drilled. As he set an eyelet, he would ascend and stand on it for footing in order to drill the next hole. Slowly but steadily, he worked until he finally reached the summit. He then secured the rope to the eyelets with knots to allow a hand-over-hand traverse. Although it was a crude device, it worked. In the days that followed, others tried Anderson's route. Being an early entrepreneur, Anderson soon began charging for tours to the top. He had dreams of erecting a wooden staircase up the backside and even building a hotel near the base. John Muir was the eighth person to reach the summit using the Anderson rope system. That same October, Sally Dutcher became the first woman to climb to the top. However, the elements took their toll on the rope until it became unusable.

By 1884 Anderson had passed on, so two young men, Alden Sampson and A. Phimister Proctor, set up a replacement rope. In 1910 the Sierra Club placed a single cable down Half Dome's slope and removed the rope. David Curry pressed for an easier route to attract more potential customers for his namesake village, Camp Curry. The Yosemite Board of Commissioners considered the idea of a wooden staircase to the top, which obviously didn't happen.

The current system of steel cables, pipe supports, and two-by-four wooden footrests set 10 feet apart was first put up by the Sierra Club in 1919. At the same time, granite steps were

Vintage photo of the single rope system circa 1917

built into the Sub Dome, leading up to the saddle at the base of the cables.

Improvements to the Half Dome trail and to the cables themselves have been made by the Park Service throughout the 20th century and continue today. In 2005, the Park Service performed extensive work on the steps of Sub Dome to make this segment safer. Weather ravages the trail infrastructure and the Park Service performs periodic maintenance. Before taking your trip, you should confirm that the trail is open and no repairs are in progress.

The cable banister today

The cables are made available for hikers' use each spring (late May) and are taken down in the fall (early October), depending on weather conditions. The entire length is comprised of three separate runs of nearly 1-inch steel cable, each anchored into the rock. The heavy steel cables are not actually taken down and off the rock; rather, they are merely laid down out of their 3-foot poles. (Heavy snow and avalanches could damage the poles if they were left up.) It would still be possible to pull yourself up the cables, but this would be foolhardy and downright dangerous.

Today, the ascent up the cables (a bi-directional "banister") allows a hiker to travel over 425 feet vertically to a point near the very top. If you're physically fit you can reach the summit in 15 minutes—that is, if you arrive early (by 11 a.m.), which will necessitate a 6 a.m. departure. Usually, on weekends soon after noon the cables are so crowded that the line of hikers resembles a very slow-moving caterpillar.

At the top, the surface consists of a few large hunks of granite at the north peak and a smooth, sloping area as big as seventeen football fields to the south. The northwest wall dominates that edge. There are only a few small trees left. Camping was allowed prior to 1992, and most of the trees were cut for firewood. Today, you cannot camp above the 7600-foot level, and marmots and squirrels appear to be the only inhabitants. These furry mammals are cute, but resist the temptation to feed them. They need to be self-sufficient and not dependent on handouts for their survival. The summit is a protected area due to the dwindling population of Mt. Lyell salamanders that live deep in the cracks on Half Dome.

With the thousands of visitors that reach the summit each year, I was surprised to find that there is no formal control over who can go up the cables. Age, size, or strength don't matter. There is no one monitoring the cables, so if you are willing, you can attempt it. Even a quota system would require park resources to manage, and there are no plans to limit access. The youngest child I've seen go up the cables was about 10. At that age, children could have the energy and spunk to make the hike, but waiting until they're a couple of years older is recommended. With an adult behind them on the cables, children are fearless. Please make a rational decision about taking children. This is a hard hike and youngsters especially need to be properly outfitted and prepared. They should be allowed to rest often and go at their pace—not yours. Water is essential for them. Turn back if it becomes too much—don't push them.

Half Dome is also known for its oft-photographed 2000-foot sheer face. Experienced rock climbers often scale it, since it is one of the world's most vertical rock walls. It was first climbed in 1957 by Royal Robbins (aged 21), Mike Sherrick, and Jerry Gallwas, taking them five days. Today, this wall and nearby El Capitan are popular climbs; however, our undertaking is a hike and not a climb. We will venture up the safer back side of Half Dome.

An Overview of the Half Dome Hike

Why would you want to hike up to Half Dome? Fair enough question. The quick answer is: "Because it's there!" Seriously,

The view to Half Dome from Clouds Rest

Mathew Grimm

View of the summit and the Visor   Michael McKay

after one has done the other challenging valley hikes, such as
Yosemite Falls or Glacier Point, there comes a time to enter
into the fraternity of those who "made it to the top," like the
gift store T-shirt says. Half Dome is a grand accomplishment.
Doing anything for 10 to 12 hours is a cause for celebration. The hike can awaken your adventuresome spirit with
a new feeling of "I can do anything." Some of the comments
I've overheard from those who've gone to the top include:
"Awesome," "Breathless," "Adrenaline Rush," and "This is the
true Spirit of Yosemite." For many people, this is their Mt.
Everest and is one of the most ambitious things they will ever
undertake. Maybe after conquering Half Dome you'll embark
on even more challenging adventures.

The Half Dome hike is a first-class adventure. You'll get a chance to get up close and personal with Vernal Fall and Nevada Fall, stroll through scenic Little Yosemite Valley, and view the crystal-clear Merced River. The long series of switchbacks on the way to the base of Half Dome are strenuous and will test your resolve to get to the top. Finally, there is the long pull up the cables, which is guaranteed to raise your heart rate. All of this will lead you to the climax: standing on the very top of Half Dome and gazing down nearly a mile onto the valley floor.

Some people do this hike in two days. They load backpacks, hike up one day, and arrive in Little Yosemite Valley to spend the night (permit required). Then the next morning they summit with a smaller daypack and return to the valley floor the same day. My preference is for a one-day hike. Carrying a 30–40 pound pack up the steep trails is quite a lot of work. Although you'll enjoy the fun of the camping experience, you'll also need to deal with bears. You'll have to carry all your food, clothing, and gear about 2000 feet up from the valley. A one-day trip is very doable. You'll get a full night's sleep, but will need an early start; 6 a.m. is recommended, with a 7 a.m. "drop-dead" start time. For a one-day trip, you will need to carry only minimal equipment, as described later. Your hike will start out chilly, but should soon warm up to be very pleasant. With increasing altitude the air will actually get cooler. If you keep a good pace, you should be heading up the cables well before noon and will arrive back to your camp before sunset.

When you're on the top, a few feet from the edge, you can look down on the Ahwahnee hotel or over at Clouds Rest, Glacier Point, El Capitan, and toward the vast San Joaquin Valley on the horizon. So this is why we do it. With conditioning and commitment, almost anyone can do it.

Leave No Trace

I highly encourage you to respect Yosemite (and other areas you frequent) so that future generations can enjoy them, too. The "Leave No Trace" principles are merely common-sense outdoor ethics to help preserve our fragile ecosystem. Leave No Trace is an awareness and an attitude, not a rigid set of rules. As more natural areas are turned into housing projects, strip malls, and parking lots, humans need places to go to take respite and contemplate the meaning of life. Keep these principles in mind:

1. Plan ahead and prepare.
2. Travel and camp on durable surfaces.
3. Dispose of waste properly.
4. Leave what you find.
5. Minimize campfire impacts.
6. Respect wildlife.
7. Be considerate of other visitors.

Hiking is a fun, rewarding, and healthy experience. You'll soon join a strong fraternity of fellow hikers. I find it interesting that folks say "hello" to a hiker as they pass on a trail, yet put up a protective shield if they see the same person in a store. Be courteous when passing others on a trail, and always let downhill hikers have the right of way on a narrow passage. They will have momentum, and yielding to them will give you a chance to rest!

2
Precautions

This is basically a very safe hike; however, a few words of caution are appropriate. Make sure you understand the challenge ahead of you. Do not attempt the hike if you are not prepared.

Intensity

Of the 23 hikes listed in the official park guide, the Half Dome hike is the only one described as "extremely strenuous." The numbers speak volumes: 15.5 miles round-trip; 10 to 12 hours in duration; 4737-foot altitude gain. Make sure that you're physically prepared for an adventure of this magnitude. You will be exerting yourself for an extremely long time, perhaps longer than you ever have before. Your first attempt at hiking Half Dome may well take you longer than 12 hours.

Weather

Summer in Yosemite is pure heaven. The days are warm, and the nights are cool. Middle-to-late summer can bring very high temperatures to the valley, and your hike will become even more challenging. It's not unusual for August temperatures to approach 100° Fahrenheit. Fortunately, clear skies generally prevail, but an occasional shower is common in any mountain environment. For the Half Dome hike, you'll be limited to the summer season, consistent with the installation of the cable system. However, the biggest concern is lightning. Storms can arise at any time of year, but they are most common during the later summer months. In August, localized hot air often meets cooler upper-layer air, creating cumulonimbus clouds and resulting in thunderstorms and lightning accompanied by heavy rains. You may be deceived, because days often start out clear and with blue skies. Slowly, clouds move in until the skies are overcast and you can hear distant thunder. Once the skies open up, storms usually last a few hours. Not only is it no fun slogging through mud, but it can be extremely dangerous. Slick and muddy footing can

Stormy weather is a serious threat

result in ankle twists and falls, but lightning can be deadly. If you hear any thunder, immediately turn around and return to the valley. Do not continue on your hike to Half Dome. The large granite rock is a giant lighting rod. Not only is the surface of the rock very slick when wet, making it nearly impossible to go up, as one of the highest structures in the area the rock attracts lightning strikes. People have been struck and have died as a result of lightning. Even if you have clear skies above, lightning can travel nearly 10 miles from its source. A permanent sign at the base of Half Dome cautions hikers not to ascend when thunder is in the area. On the very top of Half Dome is an outcropping of rock, near the northwest peak. What looks like a cave is actually a jumble

DEADLY LIGHTNING

In July of 1985 five hikers ascended Half Dome late in the day and met with tragedy from two ferocious lightning strikes. Their story is documented in the book, *Shattered Air: A True Account of Catastrophe and Courage on Yosemite's Half Dome*, by Bob Madgic (Burford Books, 2005). It recounts how the young men, full of enthusiasm and bravado, ignored nature's warnings and hiked up the famed cable trail right into the vortex of a fierce thunderstorm. They took shelter in the rock "cave" enclosure at the summit. Lightning struck the Dome twice, killing one of the hikers and causing a second to tumble over the edge, out of the grasp of his best friend. Two survivors were gravely injured. Other hikers arrived at the scene and administered emergency medical treatment for over five hours, deep into the night. Finally, an air-ambulance helicopter arrived in Yosemite Valley at 12:30 a.m., and, in a race with the descending moon, made three dangerous trips to the top of Half Dome to bring the surviving victims down.

of large rock slabs near the visor. This seems like it would be a safe haven in a storm. It's not.

If there's even a hint of thunder, lightning, or rain, get off the rock immediately and descend to a lower elevation. Repeat: do not press your luck. Be nowhere near Half Dome if there is even a remote chance of adverse weather coming in. (It will be there to hike another day!) If you cannot immediately get down to a lower altitude, insulate yourself by squatting on your pack and presenting the smallest possible target for the lightning.

Altitude Sickness

The apex of Half Dome is at 8842 feet, a height where altitude sickness is not commonly experienced. Acute Mountain Sickness (AMS) is usually only a concern well above this elevation. However, anyone who goes to altitude can experience symptoms. Susceptibility is primarily related to individual physiology and genetics, as well as to a person's rate of ascent. Age, gender, physical fitness, or previous altitude experience do not seem to be significant factors. Symptoms include headache, fatigue, weakness, dizziness, nausea, and stomach distress.

At the far end of the altitude sickness spectrum are high altitude cerebral edema and high altitude pulmonary edema. These are potentially life-threatening illnesses that usually do not occur below 12,000 feet. If you decide to follow up the Half Dome hike with an expedition to the top of Yosemite's 13,000-foot peaks or even to nearby Mt. Whitney to the south (at 14,495 feet, it's the highest point in the lower 48), then you'll need to read up on high-altitude cerebral edema and high-altitude pulmonary edema. These are serious conditions, and discussing them is outside the scope of this book. Medical science has a lot to learn about altitude sickness, as it appears to be variable for each individual. If you're concerned, you can spend a day or two in the park doing some test hikes to get acclimated. If you do experience altitude-sickness symptoms, the best cure is to descend. Drugs are rarely helpful. Getting a good night's sleep the day before the hike and drinking lots of water may reduce the onset of discomfort. In general, children are more susceptible to altitude sickness than adults. Half Dome just isn't high enough to cause problems for most people. The rule of thumb is that if you feel unwell at altitude, it is probably altitude sickness unless there is another obvious explanation. The immediate remedy is to descend.

> *If you're concerned about altitude sickness, you can spend a day or two in the park doing some test hikes to get acclimated.*

Mosquitoes

Pesky mosquitoes congregate near water sources; they commonly plague backcountry hikers. At Yosemite, their presence depends a lot on the previous winter's snow pack and on when the melt occurs. Fortunately, you will see few of the critters on this hike thanks to the wind and the lack of standing water. You may get bitten while relaxing on the valley floor. The worst times will be in the morning and at dusk, when the air and water are calm. It's a good idea to apply a repellent and wear long pants and long sleeves when in camp. An outdoor ranger talk or evening walk can be a challenge if you do not take precautions.

Ticks

In the spring, ticks become active. The species present in the park can transmit the bacteria that cause Lyme disease. Ticks prefer cool, moist environments such as shrubs and grasses; for complete protection, avoid those places. Check yourself and others periodically. Wear light-colored clothing so that the ticks stand out. It's a good idea to tuck your pants into your boots or socks. Gaiters are handy to close the gap between your boots and pants. You may also consider spraying repellant on your clothes. On the Half Dome trail you'll be walking on gravel, dirt, or stones, so the odds of picking up a tiny hitchhiker are small.

Waterborne Critters

The days of dipping your canteen into the closest stream for a refreshing drink are pretty much gone in today's world. Water contaminated with viruses, protozoa, and bacteria can cause serious illness or even death. The U.S. Environmental Protection Agency has estimated that nearly 90 percent of the world's fresh water is contaminated. Giardiasis is a concern in Yosemite. It is caused through infection of the intestine by the single-celled parasite *Giardia lamblia*.

The parasites live and reproduce in human or animal intestines. Once in the intestines, they attach to the inside of the intestinal wall, where they can disrupt the normal function of the intestines and compete for nutrients. They can survive for a long time in soil or water until they are ingested by another host. Giardia is spread by contact with the fecal matter of deer, rodents, bears, birds, and people. The risk is that you may end up with a range of discomforts including severe diarrhea. Don't assume that because you find a "natural" stream you are safe. The same goes for the sparkling waters of the Merced. Some people think that if you dip into a moving water source, it's okay to drink. Wrong. Don't do it. The giardia protozoa can cause one of the more common types of dysentery, and you may not feel the effect until 10 days after your trip. You may not even associate your illness with your hike. I had a friend who was sick for a long time. The doctors traced the possible cause to a day that he spent at Yosemite when he cooled himself off under a waterfall and swallowed some of the spray! The symptoms to watch out for include stomach pain, diarrhea, nausea, malaise, gas, and weight loss. If you suffer from these, get treatment. However, the parasite may not totally go away, and

The days of dipping your canteen into the closest stream for a refreshing drink are pretty much gone in today's world.

symptoms could erupt years later. Prevention methods such as filtration, iodine tablets, and ultraviolet water purification are recommended. While the odds of getting sick are low, it's better to be on the cautious side.

It's also a good idea to clean your hands regularly, especially after using the toilet facilities and before eating. In order to avoid spreading germs, don't touch your face. Since there's no potable water on the trail, hand cleaning is best accomplished with antibacterial wipes or gels. These are available in travel sizes and will greatly reduce the chance of illness.

The Falls

On this hike, you'll come close to two very high waterfalls. Although at 2425 feet Yosemite Falls is the tallest in North America, two impressive falls on the trail will also amaze you. First, you'll reach Vernal Fall (317 feet), then later Nevada Fall (594 feet). Both are full and flowing in the spring as the winter snow melts. Both are on the Merced River and offer great photo opportunities. If you arrive later in the summer, their flows will be quite reduced.

Sad as it is, people do go over these falls accidentally and die. Every couple of years a person disappears over a fall.

Hikers near Nevada Fall   Michael McKay

Despite safety railings, fencing, and warning signs, people are tempted to wade too close to the edge and are swept over. Rescue is nearly impossible because the volume of water in high season is tremendous. At the base of the falls, large boulders form caves that can trap a body. By late summer, the flow changes from a roaring cascade to a mere trickle. In the autumn and winter, it's interesting to view the bottom of one

A FALL BY ANY OTHER NAME

While most of us are used to calling any waterfalls "falls," there is a distinction to be noted. If the water goes over the edge straight down to the bottom without hitting rocks and getting diverted, it's called a "fall." If there are intermediary stages, it's called "falls," as in "Yosemite Falls." To confuse things even more, if you were talking about Vernal Fall and Nevada Fall together, they would be "the falls."

of the bigger falls. The jumbled collection of huge boulders confirms why immediate body recovery is very difficult. On the Half Dome hike, the waters above Vernal and Nevada Falls are inviting. Venturing out from the shore is very risky because the current can knock you over while you stand on the smooth rocks. Once a person is in the fast moving waters, it is very difficult to get out. Be respectful of the Merced!

Falling

Although most of this hike is straightforward, there are stages where you'll encounter granite steps and challenging footing. You'll be on gravel and pointed rocks that may cause you to slip or trip. Always watch where you are stepping and be in control. Take your time. You'll need to ascend three very difficult stretches: the lower Mist Trail (next to Vernal Fall), the upper Mist Trail (between Liberty Cap and Nevada Fall), and the approach just before the cables, called Sub Dome. Each of these segments comprises over 700 steps.

The origins of these trails date back to the late 1800s. A lot of trail construction was done by early settlers like George Anderson. Civilian Conservation Corps teams and other crews made many improvements and upgrades during the 1930s. Dynamite and strong backs have made the trails accessible for your enjoyment. Although upgrades, renovations and repairs of the trails are ongoing, you still need to be mindful: take your time and don't rush.

If you lose your concentration on the trail, you risk taking a nasty fall. Sprained ankles and broken bones are among the most common injuries. The biggest technical challenge is climbing up (and down) the cables on the backside of Half Dome. This will definitely give you a rush. Be advised that although it has seldom happened, people have fallen to their deaths by slipping from the cables. A 2000-foot drop looms not far from the cables. A wet surface, smooth-soled shoes, and a lost grip have been the primary causes of falls. Stay inside the cables. If a person faints or suffers a heart attack, the stanchions and other hikers may stop their descent. If you feel at all queasy or light headed, go back down.

Repairing the cables in 1934

Yosemite Museum, National Park Service

THE NAME GAME

The names of various Yosemite features have come from many sources. Some were derivatives of the native Miwok Indian names, or the substitution of suitable English names in place of the Indian. Early frontiersmen gave distinctive names of their own choosing, as it was hard to get many of the Native-American names adopted. Professor J. D. Whitney, California State Geologist in the 1860s, was responsible for some of the names, as was Dr. Lafayette H. Bunnell, the physician in the Mariposa Battalion. Bunnell learned much from the last Chief of the tribe, Ten-ie-ya, and his 1880 book *Discovery of the Yosemite* is a seminal piece. Some names were given because of the visible characteristics of certain formations. Also, popular usage and vernacular have changed names given earlier. For example, El Capitan has been known as "The Captain," "Rock Chief," and by its Indian name, "Tote-ack-ah-noo-la." The spellings are phonetic, as the Miwoks had no written language. In another example, the final granite staircase before the cables has been called "The Shoulder," "Devil's Staircase," and even "Quarter Dome." Today, the commonly accepted name is "Sub Dome."

The pull up the cables is much easier when you arrive before 11 a.m., when you should have a clear path with few people crowding you. Later in the day, I have seen queues of dozens of hikers waiting over 30 minutes to begin their ascent up the cables.

Bears and Mountain Lions

There are definitely bears in Yosemite. The grizzly bear (as seen on the California state flag) is now extinct from the state, but it's estimated that there are up to 500 black bears living within the park's boundaries. The term "black" is misleading, because the actual color of these bears varies from blond to cinnamon brown to black.

Most bears in Yosemite live far from the valley, residing in the vast backcountry. The populated valley floor provides an easy meal for wandering bears. From June to August, the bears normally eat currants, raspberries, chokeberries, and manzanita berries. When these are scarce, the bears may wander through campgrounds, looking for leftovers. Their intellect and their superb sense of smell can guide them right to the food-storage cooler in your car. Bears are not dumb animals. Cubs are often trained to climb trees to get to food bags. They recognize that boxes in the shape of coolers mean food. With males weighing up to 350 pounds, you can imagine the damage they can cause. The park displays photos of cars ripped open like a cans of sardines. Don't think you can hide food from the bears.

The best solution is the use of bear boxes in the campsites and a vigorous education program. Please heed the advice you get and help save an unwitting bear from expulsion or worse.

The National Park Service has an aggressive program to reduce human-bear contact. Bear-resistant canisters are highly recommended, and, in most places, required in Yosemite National Park. When camping in those few areas within Yosemite where bear canisters are not required, it is strongly recommended that you store your food in one anyway. Valley campers and car owners must sign a form showing that they understand the rules. The best solution is the use of bear boxes in the campsites and a vigorous education program. Please heed the advice you get and help save an unwitting bear from expulsion or worse.

It is rare that you'll even see a bear on the Half Dome trail. If you do, leave it alone. Keep at least 50 yards away. If it is aggressive and you have a cell phone, call the park's Save-a-Bear hot-

Resting up before tackling the cables   Michael McKay

line at (209) 372-0322 for the authorities to come and deal with
it. If you see a bear at your campsite, make loud noises to scare
it away. Bears are inherently shy, and they would prefer to avoid
a confrontation. Many times I have gotten up in the middle of
the night to answer nature's call only to see a lumbering bear
walking in the dark, among the tent cabins. We both ignore
each other and tend to the task at hand. Finally, never try to
play with cubs; they are cute, but momma won't like it and may
want to teach you a lesson. In reality, more people at Yosemite
are hurt by encounters with deer than with bears.

Mountain lions also live in the park. Sightings are very rare,
but be aware of their existence. Humans are not their natural
food, but the cats can be unpredictable. Don't hike alone, and
keep small children near you. If you encounter a lion, hold your
ground or back away slowly. If it appears to be threatening you,

wave your arms or hold your coat open. Your goal is to make yourself look as large and threatening as possible—but don't aggressively approach the lion. Maintain eye contact, and do not crouch down. Do not run—this will ignite the lion's hunting instincts. If you are sensing a coming attack, throw sticks or rocks at the lion. Pick up or restrain small children to keep them from panicking and running. If a mountain lion attacks, fight back!

🎞 ***3*** 🎞

Preparations

Preparation is the key to any successful undertaking. I suggest you plan your trip several months in advance. Your two "critical path" elements are (1) accommodations, and (2) conditioning. You'll need enough time to secure a place to stay. You'll also need time to gradually get in shape, get your equipment, break it in and take several practice hikes.

Getting There

Yosemite is about 200 miles east of San Francisco, California. Half Dome is at 37° 44' 46" north latitude and 119° 31' 55" west longitude. From the Bay Area, the drive is an easy three to four hours, depending on your stops and observance of speed limits. Be advised that the California Highway Patrol is one of the nation's finest and uses radar and aircraft to monitor speed.

The Los Angeles basin lies about 300 miles to the south, and visitors arrive in droves from that area as well. The drive from LA takes about six hours. The only major population center to the north and east is Reno/Lake Tahoe. Most international visitors to Yosemite will probably arrive for their vacation from the San Francisco area. I suggest you consult an online map service for precise directions and travel times from your starting point. Enter the zip code for the park as 95389.

There are four access highways into the park. These are California highways 120 (east and west), 41, and 140. They are well-maintained roads, but may be closed during winter storms. Hwy. 120 through Tioga pass can be snowbound until July.

HIGHWAY 120 WESTBOUND

From Nevada, Hwy. 120 brings visitors from Reno, Carson City, and Lake Tahoe via Hwy. 395 and the Lee Vining area directly into the northeastern part of the park. Entrance to Yosemite is via the Tioga Pass entrance. However, this road is *not* snowplowed during the winter. It often remains inaccessible through early July, so plan accordingly. Fun stops at nearby Mono Lake and the ghost town of Bodie make this route exciting. As you work your way through the park and toward the valley, be sure to catch the view of Half Dome to your left. From this perspective, it looks much different than when viewed from the valley.

HIGHWAY 41

Southern California access is from either Hwy. 99 through Bakersfield and Fresno or via Interstate 5 through Fresno. On both routes, you'll be aiming for Hwy 41. Hwy 99 usually has more slow truck traffic. The I-5 turn-off at Kettleman City onto Hwy. 41 is near the sprawling (and odiferous) Harris cattle ranch. Regardless of your route, Hwy. 41 soon becomes a scenic, rolling mountain road. Oakhurst will be your last major gas/food stop, and you can indulge yourself at the nearby Chukchansi Gold Resort & Casino. You will enter the south entrance of the park near Wawona and the Mariposa Grove, home to some of the world's biggest trees. Another bonus is that you have access to the connector road to Glacier Point. A short 40-minute drive off Hwy. 41 will take you to the vista point overlooking the entire Yosemite Valley. The view is often seen in posters of the park, as it encompasses El Capitan, Half Dome, and all the major formations.

HIGHWAY 140

The southwestern access to the park is from Hwy. 140, which follows the Merced River Canyon into the park at the Arched Rock entrance. Visitors from Central California arrive on this route, a gentle, rolling road. It crosses the famous Hwy. 49, which passes by many of the gold mining sites that thrived in the mid-1800s. This is a good diversion if you have time. A fun trip is north along Hwy. 49, which runs through many of Mariposa County's Gold Rush discovery sites. Hwy. 140 is subject to landslides near El Portal, so check on current conditions with your travel agent, the American Automobile Association, or the park's information service. There have been times in the past that it has been blocked for months.

HIGHWAY 120 EASTBOUND

Since the majority of visitors to Yosemite arrive from the west, I will elaborate on this route. After leaving the San Francisco Bay Area on interstates 580, 205, and 5, you'll soon follow the signs to Hwy. 120 and Yosemite. Upon arriving at Oakdale, you'll see the last significant collection of fast food

Cricket—gone but not forgotten

restaurants, gas stations, and strip malls. If you forgot to pack anything, this will be your chance to stock up before entering the park. You should top off your gas tank here. While there are a few gas stations before the park, the prices rise dramatically. Be forewarned—once you're inside the park, there is *no* gas available in Yosemite Valley. You should fill up here so you can make the trip back to Oakdale upon your return from your hike.

Continuing, you will soon enter the foothills of the Sierra. These are beautiful rolling hills with very rocky soil that discourages the planting of crops. Eight miles east of Oakdale, keep your eyes open on the left side for a memorial to "Cricket." Here you'll see a few wilted wreaths, placed here to honor a gray mare that once stood at the fence by the road to watch traffic. Every time I drove the route in the 1990s, Cricket would be patiently waiting to welcome us to her turf. When she died, a small sign with a metal horse figurine on top was erected, and people added flowers and wreaths in her memory.

This entire general area is known as the Gold Country, and is home to many historical sites. As you continue on Hwy. 120, you will come to the small town of Knights Ferry. Turn left down the road to visit a very interesting place. In 1848, Dr. William Knight operated a water taxi to transport gold miners across the Stanislaus River (pronounced *Stan-is-law*). This barge-like system was in effect until a bridge was constructed in 1863. Although beefed up since its construction, this is one of the oldest and one of the few remaining covered bridges in the western United States. It is the longest covered bridge west of the Mississippi. Over time, the ferry grounds came to house a sawmill, a flour mill, and a power generating station. At some point a large turbine was installed to provide electricity to the area. Ruins of this complex still exist today. The Army Corps of Engineers operates a visitor center featuring a diorama that describes the role the area played during the dynamic gold rush era. It's well worth stopping at Knights Ferry, which is a cute collection of antique stores and historic houses. If you have time, you can tour the ruins and take a white-water raft trip with one of the many outfitters in town.

Continue on Hwy. 120 and be alert for a hard right turn as the road heads east, just south of Sonora—Hwy. 108 continues straight. Watch for the Yosemite Hwy. 120 sign; you'll turn right here. If you want another enjoyable side trip, continue on

The Knights Ferry covered bridge is the longest of its kind in the West

Hwy. 108. In just a couple of miles, exit onto north Hwy. 49. You'll pass through the towns of Jamestown, Sonora, Columbia, Angels Camp, and Sutter Creek. These were all important settlements during the Gold Rush and many have been preserved. If you continue north, you can visit Coloma, the site of the first discovery of gold in the South Fork of the American River, on January 24, 1848, by James Marshall. Gold mines in this part of California once produced 24.3 million ounces of the precious metal, worth about $16 billion in today's dollars.

If you don't divert onto highways 108 and 49, be sure to turn right at the Hwy. 120 sign. This will take you directly to Yosemite without any further confusion. The next attraction you will see is an immense stack of logs that easily reaches over 80 feet high. This lumber mill is not open for tours, but you will be amazed at the neat stack, which is equipped with water sprinklers to keep fire danger down. This complex is

A huge stack of logs maintained by Sierra Pacific Industries

owned by Sierra Pacific Industries, the third-largest private landowner in the United States. The family-owned business manages 1.5 million acres of California timberlands. It produces millwork, lumber, and wood-fiber products.

Just up the road on Hwy. 120 is the very small town of Chinese Camp, which was once home to nearly 5000 Chinese immigrants, who worked the gold mines. At its peak, the camp boasted several stores, hotels, joss houses (temples), blacksmiths, a church, a bank, a Wells Fargo office, a Masonic Lodge, and a Sons of Temperance building. Few historic structures remain.

Next you will pass Don Pedro Lake, an artificial reservoir ringed by 160 miles of shoreline and containing nearly 13,000 surface acres of water. It offers a houseboat marina, a boat-launch ramp, fishing, and 172 campsites. The present shoreline of the lake was created in 1971 when the new Don Pedro Dam of the Tuolumne River was completed, replacing a dam built in 1923. The Tuolumne flows out of Yosemite.

Continuing on Hwy. 120 for 5 miles, you will arrive at a very small area known as Moccasin. There is an interesting fish hatchery here, open to the public. Called the Moccasin Creek Hatchery, it is operated by the California Department of Fish and Game and consists of eight large tanks holding fry of varying sizes; a self-serve machine dispenses a handful of feed for you to toss to the fish. These rainbow trout are released as part of the state's stocking program. I've seen monsters over 18 inches long in the tank!

At Moccasin, you can also see the historic power-generating station, a San Francisco Power and Water facility. (It's not open for tours.) In 1921, San Francisco obtained the rights to construct the Hetch Hetchy dam on the Tuolumne River to provide water and electricity to the growing city. At the power station, an engineering marvel built in the Art Deco style, you can see four 12-foot-diameter pipes that carry water over and through the mountains, nearly 200 miles to San Francisco Bay Area reservoirs for distribution. Turbines here provide power from the Moccasin plant.

Immediately after leaving the fish hatchery, you will need to make a choice of roads: to climb the Old Priest Grade or the New Priest Grade. They merge at the top of the hill, so either will work. The elevation will rise 1500 feet in this short leg. The Old Priest Grade is less than 3 miles long, and was the only road over the mountain until the new 8-mile switchback road was built. The old road is steep, exceeding a 6-percent grade. While about 10 minutes shorter, it will strain your cooling system going up and smoke your brakes on the return. I suggest the safer New Priest Grade, which is labeled

THE FIGHT OVER HETCH HETCHY

The melodious name "Hetch Hetchy" comes from a grass with edible seeds that grows in the area. Following the 1906 earthquake and the severe lack of water that contributed to raging fires, San Francisco sought a solution. The city appealed to the U.S. Department of the Interior for the water rights to the Tuolumne River in Yosemite. Following a seven-year fight by environmentalists (led by John Muir and the Sierra Club), Congress passed the Raker Act, permitting the flooding of the Hetch Hetchy Valley. In 1923, the O'Shaughnessy Dam was completed. As a result of subsequent expansion, it now reaches 430 feet high. The controversy has not ended, with many now advocating the removal of the dam to restore the pristine valley.

as Hwy. 120. Big Oak Flat and Groveland appear next and are your last stops for antiques and food. The park entrance is 30 minutes ahead.

Please drive safely. You may not be used to the mountain hairpin turns and limited visibility. Pass cautiously. Much of your travel will be on two-lane roads with sharp cliffs just feet away. If you are slower than the flow of traffic, use a turnout to let others by. Do not speed; speed limits are enforced throughout the park.

Lastly, consider taking public transportation to the park. Several bus companies service Yosemite, and taking one will help alleviate auto traffic. The Yosemite Area Rapid Transit System (YARTS) provides reliable bus transport, with scheduled stops in the Mariposa County area from Merced to the Park on Hwy. 140. This system is also useful if you visit Yosemite during the winter and you don't have chains. Service from Mono County and the eastern Hwy. 120 area is available in the summer only. Once you're inside the valley, the free shuttle-bus system can get you to most attractions.

Accommodations

There are many alternatives for rooms in and near Yosemite. Keep in mind how popular the park is (well over 3 million visitors a year), and that everyone will be competing with you for rooms. Call very early in your planning process; you can always cancel any time during the week before your reservation date, up until the final 48 hours. Web-based companies, travel agents, and AAA are all good sources to consult. Depending on your needs, you can secure a motel room, a cabin, or a tent site. Due to the magnitude of the Half Dome hike, I highly recommend in-park Yosemite Valley accommodations. You will need to be well rested for the hike and will want to eat and sleep soon after you finish. Off-park sites will add almost an hour to both ends of the hike. Delaware North Companies, Inc. operates a number of lodging facilities in Yosemite National Park under contract with the National Park Service, and they provide many accommodation options. Some accomodations can be reserved up to a year in advance. You're competing with much of the nation (and foreign visitors as well) for the dates you want. Reservations for all Yosemite overnight accommodations can be obtained by phone, at (559) 253-5635. If things ar fully booked and you are patient, you might also secure a place when cancellations come in. The park website has an excellent description of all facilities. See www.yosemitepark. com. Campers can visit www.recreation.gov or call (877) 444-6777 to make reservations. Campsite reservations become available in Yosemite five months in advance.

CURRY VILLAGE

Curry Village has a long and hallowed history from when it was known as Camp Curry. Opened in 1899 by David and Jenny Curry, it was designed as a cheap lodging option for valley visitors. Located at the far end of the valley, it is a gate-

A WATERFALL ON FIRE

One very interesting event once held at Camp Curry was the nightly "Firefall." From its initiation in 1872, at 9 p.m. each night workers above the camp at Glacier Point would begin to push burning embers over the edge to cascade down toward the rocks behind Camp Curry in an orchestrated display. The spectacle resembled a waterfall of fire. Some who saw the spectacle when they were children have told me that it was surreal, and that the glowing embers cascading down the granite looked like something from a fairy tale. The firefalls were stopped in January 1968, when the Park Service decided that they were not in keeping with the mission of the organization. The meadows were being trampled by hordes of spectators, and thefts increased during show hours. You can see the Firefall in action in the 1954 movie *The Caine Mutiny*.

way to the many of the park's eastern attractions. The horse stables, Vernal and Nevada falls, the John Muir Trail, Half Dome, and Glacier Point are all accessible from Curry Village without driving through the park. Today it offers a variety of lodgings, including 18 standard motel rooms, 100 cabins with private baths, three specialty cabins with baths, 80 cabins with central bathhouses and 427 canvas tent cabins. Curry Village boasts a grocery and gift store, eateries, an outdoor pool, bicycle and raft rentals, children's programs, a comprehensive tour/activity desk, and a mountaineering school and mountain shop.

If you are not staying in the Curry Village area, you will need to come here to get to the trailhead. There is a large parking lot at Curry for your use. Do not park in the Backpacker lot, which is reserved for permitted multi-day hikes. While at the park, I highly suggest you leave your car parked and use the free Yosemite Valley shuttle. It takes you to all the eastern Yosemite Valley destinations and, during the summer, out to El Capitan.

TENT CABINS

My recommended accommodations for your adventure are the Curry Village tent cabins. These shelters have wood frames and floors and white canvas tops and sides. They sleep two to four people and are equipped with beds, bedding, pillows, towels, and a small dresser. Each has a single light bulb (no outlets) and a wooden door with a padlock. No cooking is permitted in or near the tent cabins. Shared toilets are nearby. Men's and women's shower facilities are located in the central part of the village, and their use is included with your reservation. (If you are not staying here, you can pay to use them.) Towels are provided. The showers get crowded

Tent cabins offer economical accommodations

between 4 p.m. and 6 p.m. as day hikers come back to camp. Lines may be long, but the hot water is plentiful. Bring sandals, soap, and shampoo. For tent cabin reservations, call (559) 252-4848. Be sure to check for current rates; the prices for tent cabins are on a par with typical motel rates.

WOOD CABINS

The wood cabins are much more substantial and comfortable than the tent cabins. For visitors who prefer a little more privacy, the wood cabins can satisfy this and also provide a more rustic mood. They are in the same general area as the other Curry Village accommodations, with easy access to nearby services.

TENT CAMPING

Yosemite has 13 excellent campgrounds. Some are reservable and others are first-come, first-served. Three sites in the eastern Yosemite Valley are convenient to the hike. They are North, Upper, and Lower Pines. Another, Camp 4, is farther away and is not reservable. The Pines offer about 400 spots and are economical. Depending on your budget and ability to sleep soundly on the ground, tent camping may be for you. Be sure to follow bear-safe storage of your food and any scented items (toothpaste, cologne included). See the Bears section in Chapter 2, "Precautions."

HOUSEKEEPING CAMP

The Housekeeping area, which is a step above traditional dirt camping, is located along the Merced River. It is also a good kick-off point for the hike. The complex consists of 266 units, each holding up to six people. Structurally, there are three concrete walls, with the entrance being a sliding curtain. Each unit has two single bunk beds, a double bed, a table, chairs, a mirror, electrical lights, and outlets. You must bring your own linen or sleeping bag. A handy Laundromat is located nearby. Restroom facilities here are shared.

IN-PARK MOTELS/HOTELS

Yosemite Lodge at the Falls is a nice motel in the center of the valley. It was upgraded in 1998, and the units are comfortable and clean. This is a good, central location, offering 226 lodge rooms, 19 standard rooms and 4 family rooms. Reserve by phone at (559) 253-5635.

The ultimate luxury is The Ahwahnee. Opened in 1927, The Ahwahnee is on a par with the finest hotels and has hosted presidents and world leaders. It has 123 rooms, consisting of 99 hotel rooms (with parlors and suites) and 24 cottages. One summer, my hiking party failed to secure other lodging, so we split the cost of an Ahwahnee room—a wonderful luxury for weary hikers at the end of the day.

Many other fine accommodations are available in Yosemite, but they are too far from the trailhead for Half Dome to be practical. Tuolumne Meadows Lodge, Wawona Hotel, and White Wolf Lodge should all be considered for your future trips to other destinations in the park.

OUTSIDE-THE-PARK ACCOMMODATIONS

Motels to the east of the park are not advised since they are too far from the valley for this hike, and Hwy. 120 might be closed with snow over Tioga Pass early in the summer. All three western access routes to the park are loaded with motels. Highways 120, 140, and 41 are all home to many types of dwellings, from large complexes to quaint lodges. The problem with staying outside the park is the long drive to the trailhead. It is over 30 minutes from most western entrance gates to the valley floor, so you'll need to add that to your time. Not a fun thing to do when you're dead tired after a very long hike.

Entrance to the Park

The standard per-car entrance fee is good for seven days, with in/out privileges. Cash, personal checks, travelers' checks, and credit cards are accepted. Take advantage of the America the Beautiful passes program. These passes, available for one annual fee, provide access to and use of National Park Service, Forest Service, Fish and Wildlife Service, Bureau of Land Management, Bureau of Reclamation, Army Corps of Engineers, and Tennessee Valley Authority sites. There are several levels of America the Beautiful passes, including a senior pass; rates vary depending on the type of pass selected. Consult the Federal Recreation Pass Programs website at www.recreation.gov/recpass.jsp.

Conditioning

I suggest you begin your Half Dome training about two months prior to your trip. This, of course, depends on what regime you now follow (30 minutes of exercise per day is recommended by doctors). Advance training will allow you to build the muscle and endurance required. By starting your conditioning early, you will have time to recover from any injury prior to the hike. To successfully get to the top and not feel like a dishrag afterward, being in shape is critical. True, you

True, you might be able to just jump out of the car with no preparation and do the hike, but you'd regret it.

might be able to just jump out of the car with no preparation and do the hike, but you'd regret it. If you haven't had a physical exam in a few years, get one. Make sure your doctor gives you the green light for the hike. You'll be doing a lot

One step at a time

of stretching, twisting, pulling, and other movements that you may not be accustomed to. If you have asthma, get your doctor's okay. Be sure to bring your inhaler. If you are middle-aged or older (or young and curious), you may want to get a treadmill stress test. Medical personnel hook you up to electrodes and put you on a moving treadmill that gets faster and steeper every two minutes. Doctors are present to monitor your heart rhythm and your ability to reach a heart rate close to your calculated maximum. They also monitor your ability to return to your resting heart rate in a prescribed time.

Start your training by walking for 30 to 45 consecutive minutes. Build your sessions until you can walk about two hours at a good pace. Try to walk as if you're crossing a street with the WALK sign blinking (that is, walk briskly). If you are able to jog, progress to running 2 to 3 miles at a moderate pace (10 to 11 minutes per mile). We're trying to build up endurance. Find some hills and move your workouts there. Throw in some biking too; it's great for the legs. If you can get to a gym, a stair stepper will be your best friend. For what you'll be doing on your hike, it will give the best return on your investment. Find a local sports stadium and walk or run the steps. Try walking up the fire escape stairs in a high-rise building. This is a good workout to do while on business trips and can be done year-round. Cross training with elliptical trainers, stationary bikes, and a good step aerobics class will all help. The rowing machine is one of the best overall workouts you can get. Build up endurance and calluses (you don't want to experience blisters on the hike).

Start your training by walking for 30 to 45 consecutive minutes. Build your sessions until you can walk for about two hours at a good pace.

When you're within a month of the trip, seek out some nice long hills to hike on. The steeper, the better. I really believe that the best way to get in shape for an activity is to *do* the activity. Hike, hike, hike. Work up to 90 minutes, then to about three hours—then four, then five. Only you will know when you are ready. By the time you can hike for hours, you should be enjoying yourself and looking forward to the Half Dome adventure. Take the last few hikes with all the gear you'll be bringing to Yosemite. You should wear your boots as much as you can to get them broken in. In the last week, taper down, then do little for the three days before the hike. You need to rest up, and you don't want any injuries. During your training, surf the Internet and do a search on "Yosemite" and "Half Dome." A Google search recently yielded over 800 entries for Half Dome. There's a lot of good motivational information out there. Many people have provided records of their experiences and have uploaded great pictures. But don't just dream it—be it!

What to Bring

This will be a simple list. It's what I bring. This list is time tested. Modify it to your preferences and budget, but whatever works for you is perfect. I'll discuss what to bring in the order of importance. The categories are as follows:

1. Water
2. Food
3. Clothes
4. Other essentials

WATER

Water is the most important factor on this hike. You do not want to skimp on drinking. Dehydration will sap your energy and cause you to think irrationally. It can also have severe medical consequences. Your choices are two: bring all the water you'll need, or purify the water available along the trail.

With the first alternative, you'll need to haul up a *lot* of water. How much should you bring? I weigh about 200 pounds and I drink seven quarts in the course of the day. Women and smaller people can adjust downward. I don't like this alternative because water is heavy—about 2 pounds per quart. Why carry this extra weight for all those miles? And how do you carry it? In a backpack this weight would really cut into your shoulders, and your back would be soaked with sweat. The bladder-type backpack systems are popular but I don't like them because they add a lot of weight on your back. You can only carry a limited amount of water. After several hours your lower back may begin to ache. To hand carry two or more large bottles in a backpack will be dangerous as you navigate the many granite steps—let alone the cables. Plus, two 1-liter bottles may not be enough for your all-day hike, and the extra weight may set you off balance. No, you want freedom of

A fountain and sink at the Vernal Fall bridge provide the last potable water

movement. I recommend alternative number two, purifying the water.

In addition to the issue of *having* water is the problem of removing impurities. This can be done mechanically or chemically. (Boiling is not feasible unless you are camping.) A good-quality mechanical water treatment pump makes this chore easy and isn't very expensive. Here are the three types of mechanical devices to treat water, their functions, and their micron ratings:

1. Filter (1.0–4.0 microns)—Removes giardia, large protozoa and some bacteria.
2. Microfilter (.3–1.0 micron)—Removes microorganisms, including protozoa and bacteria.
3. Purifier (.018 micron)—Removes microorganisms, including viruses.

Read the filter's box carefully. The nomenclature can be confusing. The street name for these devices is "water filter."

However, as you can see above, the technical name implies distinct capabilities. A "water filter" does not do the job as well as a "water purifier." *Filters* can remove bacteria and protozoan cysts; *purifiers* can do this *and* remove viruses. Because of strict EPA requirements, a true "purifier" is hard to find. A 0.2-micron or less pore size is regarded as the optimum. Be sure to read the literature to make sure if giardia and other microscopic pathogens (disease-causing agents) will be removed. Giardia will be your biggest concern in Yosemite. There are many filter brands to choose from, and the sales staff at your outfitter can help you sort this out. A good unit will be lightweight and compact. Many come with a pleated cartridge filter and a bottle adaptor. You will be able to pump about one quart per minute. The life of a cartridge depends on the quality of water you're trying to filter; the cleaner the source, the longer the filter will last. Still water is better than moving water because in it the harmful elements tend to sink rather than circulate as they do in moving water.

Things to look for when comparing purifiers:

1. Type of pumping mechanism
2. Cleaning process (Filtering a gallon of bleach-diluted water does the trick.)
3. Is there an adaptor to attach the hose directly to your water bottle?
4. Taste (Does it have a taste-improving charcoal element?)
5. Size/weight (You'll add about 1 lb., but then you won't need to haul up extra water.)

I also bring a small ziplock bag to store the "clean" end of the system, so I don't get it contaminated by the wet, "dirty" stream water while carrying the filter. If your filter is clogged, it will take longer to pump the water (a sign that cleaning is needed). Follow the manufacturer's instructions on how to place the intake in the stream. You'll be amazed at the great job that these devices can do with a small water source.

The second method of treating water is chemical. Here there are many choices. These, while very effective, require time to work—sometimes nearly an hour. When you are on this hike, you need to be drinking constantly, and the wait period will slow you down. I prefer to pump my water at a source, then drink immediately to get ahead of the game. However, should you elect the chemical route, you can obtain water purification tablets, iodine tablets, and even military-grade products that eliminate giardia, bacteria, and viruses, and also remove sediment. These contain a small amount of chlorine, and enough agents to clarify and disinfect water from polluted sources. These tablets are even more effective when used in water that has been mechanically filtered.

It takes about four to six hours for your body to deplete its reserves of minerals and electrolytes, so this is one hike for which you should ingest some sort of energy product.

SteriPEN, a new product employing a hand held, battery powered ultraviolet light, has been shown to kill 99.9% of viruses, bacteria, and protozoa and may have promise for hikers. It is said be effective in as little as 90 seconds for a 32 oz-container of water.

I like to lace my water with a powdered energy drink. It takes about four to six hours for your body to deplete its reserves of minerals and electrolytes, so this is one hike for which you should ingest some sort of energy product. Dehydration will ruin your day. You may "hit the wall," have poor judgment, and be unable to continue the hike. A good-tasting fluid will encourage you to drink more often. Choosing which product you use will take some experimentation during your training period. Most are easy to carry, and I put the powdered crystals in a double ziplock bag to prevent loss. Then I add the product to my freshly treated water, about two tablespoons of powdered energy drink mix per quart. Since I carry two one-quart bottles, I try to keep a balance of one bottle of clear water and one bottle of energy drink.

Dehydration impairs human performance whenever the body's fluid level falls below 98 percent of normal. The main cause of dehydration is fluid loss through sweating. Sweating is a good process, since it releases heat generated by working muscles directly to the air. That the performance of athletes is hampered by a loss of fluids, electrolytes, and carbohydrates has been known for decades. Dehydration strains the cardiovascular system by reducing blood volume. For every liter of fluid lost during prolonged exercise, body temperature rises by 0.3° Centigrade, heart rate elevates by about eight beats per minute, and the volume of blood pumped by the heart declines by 1.0 liter per min.

"Drink before you're thirsty" is a great guideline. Your practice hikes will show you how much water you need.

"Drink before you're thirsty" is a great guideline. Your practice hikes will show you how much water you need. The old sailor's rule is that you should "pee clear." If you're voiding yellow, you are *not* drinking enough. People often ask if they can drink too much. Yes, you can, but you'd really have to make a dedicated effort. Recently, a 27-year-old woman died of water intoxication in Sacramento, CA, after participating in an ill-conceived radio show water-drinking contest. Water intoxication, or hyponatremia, occurs when water enters the body more quickly than the body can remove it, upsetting the delicate balance of electrolytes that are critical for nerve and muscle function. Pre-hydrating for the Half Dome hike is of questionable benefit, especially if you generally drink normal amounts anyway.

WATER BOTTLES

Canteen-type containers and small-mouth bottles are awkward on the trail and are very hard to refill. I prefer to take two one-quart, wide-mouthed hard plastic camping bottles. The better models have an attached screw top and are virtually indestructible. They're leak proof and can be dropped without fear of their breaking. Their wide mouth provides for a quick connection to many water treatment devices. Colored versions provide a quick way to distinguish your bottle from those of your hiking mates. I even use mine as a pillow when resting!

FOOD

The most important meal of the hike is actually the meal you have the night before. The nutrients you consume will take about 12 hours to be digested and fill your energy stores. Eat smart here and don't pig out. An emphasis on carbohydrates is advised because this is what your body uses first for fuel. But remember that the carbohydrates you eat the night before may be gone by hike time, so it's safest to balance protein, fat, and carbs and avoid anything that might cause indigestion. The Curry Village Pavilion Buffet serves an all-you-can-eat meal. Sample the offerings at the Curry Village Taqueria, Pizza Deck & Bar, Curry Ice Cream Stand, and Curry Coffee Corner. Other eateries around the park are also excellent, and you can reach them via the free shuttle bus. Don't drink alcohol until after your hike; it will actually dehydrate you, so stick to juices. Also, keep caffeine consumption down.

Bear-proof food storage boxes

Breakfast on the day of your hike will, by necessity, be abbreviated. Since nothing is open at 6 a.m., you'll need to bring your own food or stock up at the Curry Village store. Bagels, muffins, fruit, granola, trail mix, and orange juice are all available. Don't overdo it. Be sure to store your grub in the metal bear boxes provided. You may need to share with another tent, so don't put a padlock on the box.

While on the hike, you can bring a variety of foods, but lean to the carb side. You don't want to deplete your glycogen stores; the resulting fatigue will ruin your day. Avoid anything greasy or fatty. My own experiments have led me to bring seven energy bars and a treat like some trail mix, jerky, or other small, tasty item. Hard candy will provide sugar and keep your throat moist. Energy bars help deliver carbohydrates to your muscles, brain, and body systems to keep you alert and strong. Most other things will get smashed in your pack. Sandwiches will get squished. The important element is the water you'll be guzzling. You don't want to "bonk" half-way through the hike.

Be a good citizen and pack out all your trash. There are *no* trashcans along the entire route, so you must take out what you bring in. Do not dump wrappers in the toilets. This can make them impossible to clean. Also, don't toss apple cores or banana peels into the woods. Yes, they are biodegradable, but how long will it take? Let's keep Yosemite beautiful!

CLOTHES
Shoes

Your boots are "where the rubber meets the road," so to speak. Of all your pieces of equipment, nothing is more critical. If you take the time (and spend the money) to get a well-fitting, well-made pair of hiking boots, you'll be far along the way to completing this hike with little pain. Quality boots (and socks) will keep your feet dry and blister free. The time you spend walking around the shoe store will pay off later. When trying on boots, bring the socks you will be wearing while hiking. Get ankle-high hiking boots. On the Half Dome trail, you'll be walking over many hard granite steps, and stability is important to prevent foot stress and sprains. Your shoes are the heart of your hiking "machine." Depending on your interest in continuing hiking, you may want to stretch your budget and buy a pair that will also be good for hiking with a heavy pack.

Don't attempt the hike in tennis shoes. Repeat: *no tennis shoes.* Why? They're comfortable, aren't they? True, but they're very dangerous on smooth rocks. You'll get little traction on the slick incline of Half Dome. The route up the cables is worn smooth. Modern boots have "snow tire treads" that will allow you to grip the granite confidently. In addition, you'll be stepping on a lot of sharp rocks during the day, and gradually, the feel of those points will go right through to your feet. Also, tennis shoes and econo-boots offer little ankle support. A name-brand pair of lightweight hiking boots is recommended. You don't need "expedition" quality, but you'll be much happier investing in good shoes. They'll last for years, and you can amortize the cost over many seasons of hiking.

I've seen many people in tennis shoes and even a few in sandals, but I saw it all when I came across a woman doing the hike barefoot with duct tape wrapped over the balls of her feet.

Look for water-repellent uppers; they will keep your feet dry when crossing streams or in heavy downpours. The shank of the boot is the inner foundation that lies under your foot. Shanks come in many types. The steel shank is popular, offering protection to your sole and arch, but steel is subject to corrosion if you have not sealed your boots properly. Nylon and fiberglass shanks won't rust and are not as sensitive to temperature extremes as steel, and, as an added benefit, they are lighter than steel. Nylon and fiberglass are typically found in higher-priced boots. At the bottom of the line are fiberboard shanks. As you can guess, they're found in very low-end boots and are not recommended.

In recent years, Vibram has become the standard for soles for shock protection and long wear. With every season, new materials are being introduced. Cosmetic features, such as leather and nylon mesh, allow for a stylish look. We haven't even talked about welts, midsoles, heel counters, or lacing systems. Here is one time I trust the salesperson. Concentrate on the fit, and take your time when shopping. Most good outfitters should have an inclined board to simulate downhill walking. Remember that the second half of the hike is downhill and allow for room in the toe box so your toes don't bang against the end. If the fit is too tight, you could end up with black toenails. As you can see, shopping for a good pair of boots can be overwhelming.

Buy boots early and break them in. Take care of your boots, and they will last a long time. Be sure to seal them with the proper treatment chemicals if they are leather. Clean any mud and dirt off them before storing them, and keep them in a cool, dry place to prevent mildew from setting in.

I've seen many people in tennis shoes and even a few in sandals, but I saw it all when I came across a woman doing the hike barefoot with duct tape wrapped over the balls of her feet. No kidding. I don't know if her boyfriend had her shoes in his pack, but this was a first!

Socks

I suggest that you use a thin, wicking silk inner sock with a medium-weight hiking sock. This will reduce friction and the chances of a blister. Use this same sock combination when you try on your boots, prior to buying them. You'll be much happier if you buy several pairs of socks at the same time so that you can rotate them. "Real" hiking socks from your equipment outfitter are recommended. Stay away from using that old pair of basketball socks or tube socks. Hiking socks are engineered (yes, even socks) to provide comfort, sweat wicking, and attention to typical foot hot spots. Keeping your feet dry is the key to avoiding blisters. I like to bring spare socks in my pack, and routinely change socks on the summit for the long hike down. Bringing a spare pair will also be useful if your primary pair gets wet on the Mist Trail.

Shorts

Wear lightweight shorts; you don't need heavy weight. Baggy gym shorts are fine. You won't be needing pockets. Loose shorts allow you to move freely and should be made of polypropylene or nylon. Chafing can be a problem, so you may want to use a lubricating gel on your inner thighs.

Shirt

I prefer a long-sleeved polypropylene shirt. Polypropylene dries fast, while cotton will be clammy. The day may be chilly in the morning, but the summer sun will soon make it pleasant. You can keep your sleeves down in the early morning and fold them up as the day goes on or keep them down for sun protection. A collar will protect your neck from the intense sun later in the day. The standard button-front shirt allows you to open it up for quick cooling. What you wear depends a lot on when you go. June and October trips can be very cold at 6 a.m. The problem is that you must carry everything with you. T-shirts are tempting, but they provide no warmth in the early morning and will be soaked with sweat within a few hours. Also, the long-sleeved shirt provides a pocket or two to hold your energy bar or small camera. Many days it is windy and brisk on Half Dome, so the long-sleeved shirt is very handy for cutting the chill.

Hat

You'll need some sort of sun-shading hat. Luckily, much of the hike is in tree shade, but in the last hours to the summit you will be vulnerable to harmful UV rays, so a sun hat is another clothing item that you'll appreciate. Although the hike is balanced between sun and shade, the midday sun can be taxing in the thin air. A baseball hat is adequate and can be quickly tucked into your waist when you want to cool off your head a bit. You may consider bringing a cap-keeper strap, a clip device that secures your cap to your collar to prevent a strong breeze from pulling your hat off.

OTHER ESSENTIALS

Blister Pack

Most outfitters and drug stores will have a selection of blister-prevention products. These are friction-resisting pads, which are best if applied before you get a blister. Once a blister surfaces, you'll have to go to into mitigation mode. Moleskin is great for isolating the blister. I also carry a small tube of anti-septic ointment, just in case. In the morning before the hike, I put an adhesive blister pad on any hot spots and smear some blister-preventing petroleum jelly on the balls of my feet, my heels, and my toe edges.

Facecloth

I find that I'm sweating heavily by the time I'm halfway up the Mist Trail. Relying on a shirt sleeve for wiping off sweat doesn't seem to work. I like to carry a small white cotton facecloth, which I simply loop under my fanny pack belt so it dries as I walk. A bonus is that if you keep a corner of it dry, it's great for cleaning your glasses.

Sunglasses

Stark white granite surfaces can be very hard on your eyes. The light bounces off them and can cause fatigue. A good pair of UV-blocking polarized lenses is best for eliminating the glare. If you wear glasses, I suggest using clip-ons rather than trying to switch between your clear lenses and a pair of sunglasses. If your glasses are loose fitting, consider a strap to secure them to your head.

Trekking Poles/Gloves

Trekking poles (also known as hiking poles) are gaining popularity in the United States. Although a tree-branch hiking

The author fully geared for the ascent

stick may be handy, who wants to carry an extra 4 pounds? Poles, which have been used widely in Europe for a long time, are much lighter and work better. It's said that about 5 percent of the work of hiking is transferred from the legs to the upper body when using poles. The poles will help you up the hundreds of granite steps, as well as provide stability on the downhill. The best solution to the stress of hiking is the use of telescoping poles that adjust to your height. For optimum efficiency, the poles should be placed so that the elbows are at about hip level with not less than a 90-degree bend in the elbows. While traveling uphill, you can make the poles shorter and, conversely, while going down, you can extend them. Adjustment is easy with a simple twist motion. Using poles can be a bit awkward at first. To help you understand the proper way to use them, I refer you to a great website focused on trekking-pole technique: www.AdventureBuddies.net.

Trekking poles are better than ski poles, since they're adjustable and are much lighter. The poles have replaceable carbide tips, which grip the walking surface.

I also suggest using bicycle gloves with your trekking poles. Not only will these prevent blisters from your pole grip or straps, but they'll be invaluable when going up the cables. Bring Velcro straps to affix the poles (collapsed) to your pack when you're going up the cables.

Fanny Pack/Daypack

You'll need a container to carry all your necessities. What's best is a compact, waist-mounted fanny pack, so-called because it rides above your hips and near your center of gravity. It should have pouches to hold your water bottles and a small central pouch for food and supplies. Make sure you get a pack that can carry two one-quart plastic water bottles. (Do not use the smaller bicycle bottles. You'll need all the water you can get.) I bring my water pump to refill along the trail.

Although I see a lot of daypacks, I personally do not use one for this hike. They get too hot on your back, and you'll be sweating profusely all during the hike. The distribution of weight may cause you back strain, and the load my tip you off-balance, which can cause neck and lower back strain. Another drawback is that using a daypack makes it hard to get to your water easily. If you have to stop and remove your pack to get a drink, you may not hydrate as often as you should. The fanny pack will allow you to easily remove your bottles from their holsters while you are on the move. Opinions vary on the daypack versus fanny pack debate. I suggest you try both and decide what works best for you.

Rain Gear

There is always a chance that it will rain during the months when the cables are up. While a good drenching may sound inviting when it's hot, if you get wet and chilled while hiking, your resistance may suffer and you may not feel at your peak. You need to beware of hypothermia. If you take the Mist Trail next to Vernal Fall in early summer, you may get soaked within an hour of the start; in fact, you *will* get wet during the early season. How much depends on the amount of snow runoff. Here are two cheap and easy suggestions for keeping dry: (1) Bring a black garbage bag with holes cut for your head and arms, or (2) bring a cheap poncho from a surplus store. You can stuff either one into your pack and put it on before you enter the Mist Trail. I also suggest bringing two grocery produce bags and rubber bands to cover the tops of your boots. This will keep your feet dry. They can get very wet, otherwise. There are over 700 steps here, and the mist (or shower) off the fall pervades the upper half of the trail. You want to stay dry, but you don't want to carry a bulky jacket the entire day. Often, I can give my used rain outfits to others coming down the trail, so I don't have to carry them the rest of the day. Do *not* discard them on the trail. If you get no takers for your rain outfits, stuff them back into your pack. You will need them again if you encounter an afternoon rainstorm.

If you take the Mist Trail next to Vernal Fall in early summer, you may get soaked within an hour of the start; in fact, you will get wet during the early season.

Cell Phones

If you are communication-dependent, you'll find that mobile phone coverage is hit or miss. Some providers connect, but most users don't find service in this mountain environment. While it is very hard to connect in the valley, I have found that most people are able to call home when they're sitting on the top of Half Dome. You might want to make quick call to say: "Guess where I am; I made it!" I surmise that the direct line-of-sight path to cell towers in the San Joaquin Valley provides access. Also, many cellular companies are now using satellites to relay calls. A cell phone is a big asset in case of emergencies. As an aside, please don't bring walkie-talkie, two-way radios. First, in the mountains, reception is very spotty. Second, they are noisy. Third, they are quite annoying to hikers who are there for the serenity. And why are you separated from your party, anyway?

Emergency Supplies

Be sure to find room for a few safety items. Carry a small, two-AA-cell flashlight. June provides the maximum daylight, but hikers in August and September will find the sun setting much earlier. Remember that the sun will appear to set before the published time because of the high mountains and heavy tree cover. The hike is no fun in the dark and can be downright dangerous if you're unprepared. Also, pack a basic first-aid kit. You never know when a blister will erupt or when that hot spot will turn into a raw abrasion. Include moleskin or a similar protectant. Antiseptic, tape, band-aids, aspirin, etc. should be included. Preconfigured hiking or biking first-aid kits are perfect. A small pocket knife will be handy. I prefer the type with tiny scissors and multiple tool attachments. To be really prepared, you could throw in a compass, maps, space blanket, waterproof matches, and candles.

You'll be doing this particular hike on a well-marked trail, hopefully in less than 12 hours, but it is wise to be ready for the unexpected, depending on the time of year, weather, your starting time, injuries en route, and the like. If you do encounter trouble and are unable to move, send word down with another hiker to dispatch help. Cell phones can be used to dial (if there's reception) 911 for aid.

Suntan lotion—Apply a good coating of protection on your arms, neck, and face before beginning the hike. Bring a small sampler-size tube for a midday reapplication.

Lip balm—Your lips will welcome the relief in this dry altitude. The balm also can double as your quick suntan lotion, since most are now SPF 15.

Camera—The smaller, the better. Bulky cameras will get in your way, and you need both of your hands free. Having something around your neck will be a burden. Pocket-size digital cameras are ideal. Extra memory sticks and batteries will enhance your success.

Toilet paper—Practice the old motto, "Be prepared." Camping stores carry small rolls that are not much bigger than a roll of quarters and will easily fit into your pack. The trail toilets at Yosemite are well stocked, but heed this advice for those unpredictable times. Never soil within 200 feet of a water source or camp area, and dig a "cat hole" as appropriate.

Bicycle gloves—These are the fingerless, padded gloves that you can buy at any bike store. They're great for preventing blisters caused by your trekking poles and are perfect for pulling up the cables.

Finally, toss your sleeping bag into the car in case the nights in the valley turn cold. Bring whatever you need to get a good night's sleep—don't forget your earplugs, eyeshades, and balaclava (for head warmth).

A word about pets: The National Park Service has prohibited pets on trails for many years. In Yosemite pets are allowed only in developed areas, in some campgrounds, and on fully paved trails and roads, and they must be leashed. A kennel is available in Yosemite Valley.

Checklist

I suggest that you copy this list and go through it as you pack. Author's confession: On a recent trip, my group got halfway to Yosemite and I realized I had forgotten to pack my boots! They were hidden under the bumper of my car in my garage, and I didn't see them when I was packing. Home was a good two hours away, and traffic was getting worse each mile. The night before leaving, I had mentally gone over what I needed to bring and must have skipped over the boots. We had to stop at an outdoor store for me to buy a new pair. Use the checklist!

Half Dome Checklist

- ☐ bicycle gloves
- ☐ blister pack
- ☐ boots
- ☐ camera
- ☐ energy bars/drink
- ☐ eye mask/earplugs
- ☐ facecloth
- ☐ fanny pack
- ☐ food
- ☐ first-aid kit
- ☐ hat
- ☐ lip balm
- ☐ park map
- ☐ rain gear/gaiters
- ☐ sandals
- ☐ shirt
- ☐ shorts
- ☐ sleeping bag
- ☐ small knife
- ☐ socks
- ☐ sunglasses
- ☐ suntan lotion
- ☐ this book
- ☐ toilet paper
- ☐ toiletries
- ☐ trekking poles
- ☐ Velcro straps
- ☐ water
- ☐ water bottles
- ☐ water treatment

Youth Involvement

America is blessed to have such organizations as the Girls Scouts and Boy Scouts. These groups provide direction and a moral example, and they also build character and skills for

Serenity abounds in Little Yosemite Valley alongside the Merced River

success in the real world. Millions of kids participate in these programs. At a time when nearly 70 percent of America's schoolchildren cannot pass a physical fitness test, it's good to know that the Girl and Boy Scouts help youth appreciate the value of being fit. Both the Sierra Club and the Yosemite Association have great programs to involve our country's future leaders. Hiking in general, and the Half Dome hike in particular, are great outlets for our youth.

The *Boy Scout Handbook* is now in its 11th Edition (first-published in 1910), and is a great resource for adults as well as for young people. Its sound principles and guidance are universally applicable to all outdoorspeople. To obtain a merit badge in the field of hiking (one of over 120 possible), scouts must complete five 10-mile hikes and one continuous 20-

mile hike. The hiking merit badge is a mandatory selection in the process of qualifying for the coveted Eagle Scout rank. Though the Half Dome hike is nearly 16 miles long and not 20, because of its difficulty it is a strong candidate to satisfy the 20-mile requirement, and may be approved by the Merit Badge counselor.

To guide Scouts, the Boy Scout organization promotes a list of items useful to all hikers. Some items on the list may not apply to the Half Dome hike, but you should be aware of this information. Below is the list of the 10 Scout "Outdoor Essentials."

1. Pocket knife
2. First-aid kit
3. Extra clothing
4. Rain gear
5. Water bottle
6. Flashlight
7. Trail food
8. Matches and fire starters
9. Sun protection
10. Maps and compass

When to Go

When's the best time to go to Yosemite? For hiking Half Dome, you can forget winter, early spring, and late fall. During those times it can snow in the valley, so just getting there could be a challenge. The major consideration is: "When will the cables be up on Half Dome?" They are usually up once the snows stop (May–early June), and they are taken down in the fall (October). The exact dates vary with the weather. Personally, I prefer going in June because (1) after being inside during winter, it is a nice trip to look forward to,

(2) the days are longest in June and allow plenty of daylight to complete the hike, (3) the waterfalls are full flowing and spectacular, (4) there is less chance of a lightning storm early in the summer, and (5) the park seems to be less crowded than later in the summer, when people take their long vacations.

༄ *4* ༄
Hiking
Half Dome

I use Curry Village as "base camp" for the hike, since it is the most convenient sleeping and parking area. The often-published distance for the Half Dome hike is about 17 miles. Of course, the actual distance depends on where your starting point is and which route you take. The "zero" marker for my discussion is the logical start of the trail, next to the Merced River at Happy Isles. My cumulative distances and estimated hiking times are measured from there. I go from the trailhead to the Vernal Fall Bridge, up the Mist Trail, between Liberty Cap and Nevada Fall, through Little Yosemite Valley, then on to Half Dome. The return is via Nevada Fall and the John Muir Trail. Total distance is 15.5 miles this way, and not the 17 miles mentioned above. (This is explained a little later.) If you are staying anywhere other than in the general Curry Village area,

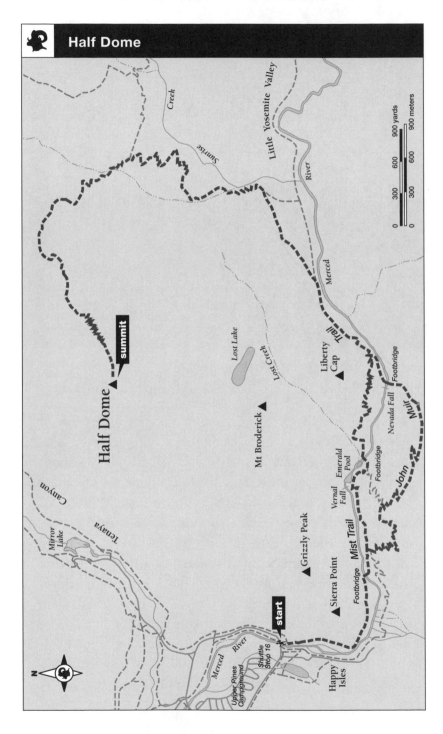

Half Dome

you'll need to get to Curry Village and walk to the trailhead. You could take the Yosemite shuttle from anywhere in the park and get off at stop number 16, Happy Isles. The big problem with this is that the shuttle buses don't start running until 7 a.m.

My pace is for a 10.5-hour round trip and this is the basis for the estimated times. Remember that time resting, enjoying the summit, and other diversions will affect your hike's actual duration. I've selected several Points of Interest (POI), which are worthy stopping points and also will help you gauge how you're progressing. You may want to use a running chronograph as a general gauge for measuring how far it is between Points of Interest. During the preparation of this guide, I used a hand-held Global Positioning System (GPS) receiver. This device allowed me to compile the trail measurements listed in the following sections. For your hike of Half Dome, I've done all the work; you do not need to bring a GPS. However, you may want to gain experience with your unit, and you can cross-check my readings. Altitudes may vary depending on just exactly where I hit the "waypoint" button. Also, I'm over 6 feet tall; very accurate altitudes would be measured at ground level. The distances in this section were compiled off the GPS also. They are not as-the-crow-flies measurements, but rather include actual odometer distances covered as I

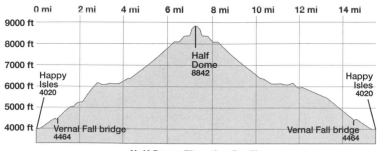

Half Dome Elevation Profile

wound through the many switchbacks. The actual direct distance from Happy Isles to the top of Half Dome is less than 2 miles, but we will need to follow the trail on a counterclockwise route to reach our goal.

If you are traveling with four or more companions, it will be difficult for everyone to stay together. We all walk at different rates, anywhere from 2 to nearly 4 miles per hour, depending on the incline and on conditioning. Agree on a plan to meet up every hour, or at the POIs described in this chapter. Make sure everyone has access to enough water, whether they carry it or pump it. If you are taking small children, keep them close to you at all times. Have a plan for them if they do get separated from you. Tell them it's best if they just stay where they are and ask other hikers for help. Giving them a whistle,

GPS PRIMER

In 1978, the United States initiated the Global Positioning System (GPS), primarily as an aid to military operations. The GPS system is a network of 24 satellites orbiting the earth at 12,000 miles out. In the 1980s, the government made the system available for civilian use. Contact with at least three satellites is needed to calculate a two-dimensional position (latitude and longitude) and to track movement. With four or more satellites in view, a modern receiver can determine the user's three-dimensional position (latitude, longitude, and altitude) as well as track movement. From this, other information, such as speed, bearing, trip distance, distance to destination, sunrise/sunset times, and other data can be calculated. Modern GPS units take advantage of hardware and software advances to yield accuracy of less than 20 feet even under dense foliage, in steep ravines, and in urban "canyons."

just in case, is a good idea. Make sure they are carrying your name and contact information, preferably attached to their clothing.

In the sections that follow, I'll describe the trail and 16 of my favorite "Points of Interest" (POI). For each one I give you the altitude, cumulative distance, and elapsed time and distance from the trailhead. My times are only guidelines and may not apply to your hike. However, this information may be useful as another data point for you. The trail map on page 70 gives you a visual of your day, and the table on page 74 lists time, elevation, and mileage for the POI's.

Starting at Curry Village

Arise early and get organized—it helps to lay out your gear the night before. Use your checklist to make sure you don't forget anything. Have your breakfast and be on the trail by 6 a.m. A good goal is to arrive at the cables by 11 a.m. to avoid the crowds. An early start will allow you to make this an easy hike at your own pace, resting as you go along. Keep in mind this a fun hike—not a death march! Remember, your pull up the cables will be much easier if you can zip right up rather than inching up in traffic.

Hike east through the tent cabins until you are next to the service road that the shuttle bus travels on. (Cars aren't allowed on this road.) You want to head toward Happy Isles. As you approach the Merced River, look to the right, and you'll see the shuttle-bus stop and a restroom facility. There will be many toilets farther on, so don't panic. This is a good place to fill your water bottles.

Continue down the service road and turn right just after crossing the Happy Isles bridge. You'll now be walking next to the river. The trail along the left side of the Merced River

POI No.	Point of Interest	Elapsed Time	Altitude Feet	Cumulative Mileage
1	Mileage marker sign	0:00	4093	0
2	Vernal Fall Bridge	0:30	4464	1
3	Top of Vernal Fall	1:00	5062	1.6
4	Silver Apron Bridge	1:10	5204	1.8
5	Little Yosemite Valley	2:00	6095	4.8
6	Half Dome-John Muir Trail split	2:50	7000	5.1
7	The Little Spring	3:10	7228	5.9
8	View of Half Dome & Sub Dome	3:35	7708	6.5
9	Base of the cables	4:30	8402	7.1
10	Apex of Half Dome	5:00	8842	7.2
11	The Little Spring—again	6:45	7228	8.5
12	Little Yosemite Valley—again	7:45	6095	10.7
13	Junction of Mist and John Muir trails	8:20	5950	11.7
14	Nevada Fall Bridge	8:30	5977	11.9
15	Vernal Fall Bridge—again	9:53	4464	14.5
16	Mileage marker sign—again	10:30	4093	15.5

will continue for 100 yards, until you are just across from the Happy Isles area. On the riverbank you will see a water-flow measuring station. The expanse well behind this area was the site of the large rock fractures caused by rock slides, as discussed in the introduction. Just to the left, you'll see the trail heading into the hills. You are now at the start of the famous John Muir Trail. Begin the hike in earnest. There will be many people on the trail, so you won't get lost. Soon you'll come upon your first picture opportunity: the mileage marker sign.

POI 1	**Mileage marker sign**
	Elapsed Time. . . . . 0 hours
	Altitude. . . . . 4093 feet
	Cumulative Distance. . 0 miles

As you head up the trail, you'll very quickly see a large red sign on your left, listing the mileage to many park destinations. (The sign was moved up the hill recently from its historic place closer to the river, although the numbers were not changed.) The Half Dome hike is listed as an 8.2 mile one-way journey. Thus, a round-trip would be 16.4 miles. This is true if you bypass the Mist trail both ways and stay on the John Muir Trail until you divert to the Half Dome trail. Your return would be on the John Muir Trail as well, totally bypassing the Mist Trail route. **The most scenic hike, and the way I recommend, is via the Mist Trail when going up and on the John Muir Trail past Nevada Fall when returning, for 15.5 miles total.** The return route is longer, but your knees will be spared the steps of the Mist Trail. I strongly feel that the hike is actually easier going up since you are primarily using your leg muscles that have been conditioned for the hike. Downhill hiking places great strain on your knees. There's only so much you can do to strengthen the muscles supporting the knees. Trekking poles help in this regard, but I will trade the slightly longer route to skip the downhill Mist Trail. Even if your knees are not a problem, the Mist Trail is more hazardous negotiating the damp steps downward. The John Muir Trail affords you vistas of Liberty Cap, Half Dome, and Nevada Fall that you would miss if you took the Mist Trail both ways.

At the mileage sign, you'll also be able to see how far it is to other destinations, such as Tenaya Lake and Clouds Rest. Save these destinations for future hikes. Did you catch the

The mileage marker sign

typo on the sign? It appears the carpenter wasn't briefed on the proper names for Vernal *Fall* and Nevada *Fall* (they should not be plural). The John Muir Trail can be used to take the multi-day route down to Mt. Whitney, a trip of over 200 miles. This is a superb trip, and is only done by those with plenty of free time (and a strong back).

Leaving the mileage sign, continue up the trail. Many people are going only to Vernal Fall, and you'll soon leave them behind. But expect to see dozens more crowding this part of the trail on your return at the end of the day.

POI 2	**Vernal Fall Bridge**
	Elapsed Time......... 30 minutes
	Altitude............... 4464 feet
	Cumulative Distance.. 1 mile

Standing on the bridge, you can look up and to the left to see the waterfall framed by trees. Early in the season, the water will be flowing strong. If you visit in the late summer, most of the runoff will be gone, and the flow will be weaker. Even mighty Yosemite Falls often dries up by late August.

This will be your last chance to use a real, flushing, porcelain toilet and running water. An emergency telephone is nearby. A sink and water fountain provide the final opportunity to fill your bottles with tap water. For the rest of the hike, you'll need treated water. As you begin the upward trail, you will pass Register Rock. For a period in the 1860s a toll was collected for passage; visitors would inscribe their names on the rock. George Anderson was a driving force in getting a trail constructed to the top of the fall.

From here, you begin the hike up the Mist Trail—so named because of the spray you will encounter as you are walking

The bridge over the Merced, below Vernal Fall

next to the Merced River. The Mist Trail parallels the Merced. Early on you'll come to a decision point: to continue up the Mist Trail or take the offshoot trail to the right left and toward Nevada Fall. The latter trail will link up with the route to Little Yosemite Valley and on to Half Dome, but is a bit longer, The main reasons for going the longer way are that it is not as steep and that it is dry. The Mist Trail in early summer can be a deluge, with the fall throwing off a shower onto the trail. It is very exciting and highly recommended. Watch for rainbows as the mist hits the sun. With your rain gear, you'll be dry enough. Halfway up, an overhanging rock arch provides a brief shelter. Your trekking poles will steady your climb—there are over 700 steps on this segment of the Mist Trail! As you approach the very top, you'll ascend several steps carved into the rock. Grab onto the convenient handrail as you complete this leg.

View of Vernal Fall from the bridge

The Mist Trail

The stone stairs and railing to Vernal Fall today

Vintage photo of the same scene, probably taken in the 1930s

Yosemite Museum, National Park Service

Top of Vernal Fall
Elapsed Time.......... 1 hour
Altitude............... 5062 feet
Cumulative Distance.. 1.6 miles

The viewing area here is superb. Fences will prevent you from accidentally going over, so you can safely snap several action shots. You can also glimpse your fellow hikers struggling up the Mist Trail. Take a rest here; you deserve it. Rejoin the trail by following the signs and go parallel to the river upstream, keeping it on your left. The Emerald Pool is inviting, but you cannot go into the water here—it is strictly prohibited. You'll soon see a wooden restroom facility off to your right. The toilets are well maintained and clean, so do your part to keep them that way.

Silver Apron Bridge
Elapsed Time.......... 1 hour 10 minutes
Altitude............... 5204 feet
Cumulative Distance.. 1.8 miles

The trail gets a little scattered, but stick to the worn path. Soon, you'll cross the river via a wooden bridge known as the Silver Apron Bridge. The river tends to run fast through the narrow channel here. Although there is an inviting chute, resist the temptation to go for a water slide ride. Remember the waterfall downstream? Entering the water is prohibited. Enough said.

Continuing on the trail, you'll soon be able to see Liberty Cap to your left (and up). You'll be having a nice walk now, on mostly level ground—in and out of the trees. Soon you'll come near a wide area that was once the site of a small hotel called La Casa Nevada, which burned down in 1891. There

Granite steps between Liberty Cap and Nevada Fall

are no artifacts to see. Get ready for a spectacular view of Nevada Fall on your right.

You're now starting to gain altitude. Your proximity to Nevada Fall provides a nice breeze to cool your sweaty brow. As you proceed up, this area may remind you of the steep steps of the Mist Trail next to Vernal Fall. Large granite switchbacks seem to go on forever. As you gaze up at row after row of steps, you appreciate the work it took to build these trails. You are now nestled between Liberty Cap and Nevada Fall. This leg is slow going, so rest occasionally and enjoy the view of Nevada Fall. Finally, you reach the top and rejoin the John Muir Trail coming from Nevada Fall.

At this point, you are over 2 miles from Yosemite Valley and less than 5 miles from Half Dome. The trail junction draws a healthy crowd of hikers in line at the composting toilet; the park does a good job of keeping the toilets on the trail clean and well stocked with toilet paper. From here, you'll head out toward Little Yosemite Valley.

The first view of Nevada Fall

POI 5

Little Yosemite Valley
Elapsed Time......... 2 hours
Altitude.............. 6095 feet
Cumulative Distance. . 4.8 miles

The trail now eases to a gentle walk in the park. You soon enter a lightly wooded area on a clearly marked trail. Don't wander off the trail, because this will accelerate erosion. Occasionally look up to your left; you'll see your goal: Half Dome. In Little Yosemite Valley, you should stop and enjoy the Merced River. Here, it is crystal clear; you can even see fish darting under logs. This is a great place to refill your water bottles. You'll have only one more chance before Half Dome, so drink what you still have and replenish both bottles. Don't be tempted to drink directly from the clear, babbling brook. Remember the giardia discussion? Be wary of the Steller's jay, an aggressive species of bird that lives in this part of the park and will take a sandwich right out of your hand. Get back on the main trail and be advised that the last field toilet is here on

The pristine waters at Little Yosemite Valley

Half Dome peaking out, beckoning

your right. Don't be tempted to camp here without a permit. After leaving this beautiful valley, the hike will get serious. Watch for the trail to fork. Right will take you to the large camping area and a ranger's camp. Go left, and you'll begin the slow steady grind uphill. The trail soon begins a series of gentle switchbacks, taking you in and out of trees. You'll be taking your sunglasses on and off, but generally, this is not a sunny hike. Just get in a groove with your trekking poles and enjoy nature at its best. Smell the Jeffrey pines, the white firs, and cedars.

Half Dome–John Muir Trail Split
Elapsed Time. . . . . 2 hours 50 minutes
Altitude. . . . . 7000 feet
Cumulative Distance. . 5.1 miles

The endless series of switchbacks continue upward at a steady pace. Don't veer off the main trail and onto any one of several false trails. Be alert; it will be easy to mistakenly take the trail to Cloud's Rest. Watch for the reassuring metal sign leading you toward a leftward path to Half Dome. Continuing, you'll see a sign indicating you have less than 2 miles to go. The trail compass bearing is 330 degrees, so you're almost due north and circling around the back of Half Dome.

The Little Spring
Elapsed Time. . . . . 3 hours 10 minutes
Altitude. . . . . 7228 feet
Cumulative Distance. . 5.9 miles

About an hour out of Little Yosemite Valley, a welcome sight appears on the left side of the trail. If you are busy talking or gazing down at your shoelaces, you may miss it. I am speaking of the last water opportunity before the dome: the Little

Your last pumpable water source—the Little Spring

Water trickles out of the spring, but is adequate

Spring. To the left of the trail, watch for two tall trees form-
ing a V. The right tree has lost its top; this will help you spot
it. You may see a few people gathered around; upon closer
inspection, you'll see water slowly running out of the earth
into a shallow 3-foot wide "puddle." Don't expect to soak your
feet here. The water lands in a hole that often is only a few
inches deep. You may see many people here directly filling
their bottles thinking it's a safe natural spring. Maybe yes,
maybe no. Remember the warnings about giardia. It seems
very possible to me that the droppings of an animal could
work their way through the soil and into the "spring." The soil
probably has not had time to filter out impurities. Treat your
water. When pumping your water, it helps if a companion
holds the intake just below the surface so you can avoid suck-
ing up the sediment from this shallow hole. You can count
on water being available here—I have hiked as late as mid-
October and been pleased to find it flowing. I suggest you
drink heartily here, then refill your bottles before continuing.
I always plan on drinking one bottle from here to the top of
Half Dome and the second bottle for lunch and for the trip
back down. This lasts me until I reach the Little Spring again
for another refill. Finish your rest stop, have a small bite to
eat, then continue.

POI 8	**View of Half Dome and Sub Dome**
	Elapsed Time......... 3 hours 35 minutes
	Altitude.............. 7708 feet
	Cumulative Distance.. 6.5 miles

You continue on a series of switchbacks, in shade of
the forest. Fallen trees that once blocked the trail have been
sawed to permit passage. When you emerge from the trees,
you will finally see the profile of the backside of Half Dome in
full. You have now gained enough altitude to see many of the
surrounding formations. This section of the trail is mellow.

You're getting close. Next stop: Half Dome

The flat area is referred to as the shoulder. Enjoy the respite, for Sub Dome is next.

One of the most difficult parts of the trail is now in front of you—Sub Dome. Sub Dome is barely mentioned when people speak of the Half Dome hike, because the challenge of the cables always gets top billing. But the Sub Dome stretch consists of over 800 granite steps of varying sizes. Some are just few inches tall, others are nearly a foot high. The actual total vertical rise is about the same as the trek up the cables. The trail twists precariously and care must be taken. This imposing area is actually part of the bigger Half Dome rock, but because it is much smaller, it is often not given as much respect. It is a very strenuous stretch. It consists of an almost endless succession of tight switchbacks of white granite. The trail was recently upgraded and is as good as it's going to be.

The Sub Dome knee grinder

There is no handrail, and it is bi-directional. Most steps are narrow and require single file passage. Move over and let the downhill hikers by. This is another area where trekking poles shine, but you'll still be very tired when you reach the top of Sub Dome.

Once at the top of Sub Dome, you can gaze down into the saddle of Half Dome and then up to get a good view of the famous cables. If you've kept pace, it should be about 11 a.m., and you'll be rewarded with finding a reasonable number of other hikers on the cables. If you have arrived after noon, you'll probably see much congestion. By 1 p.m., you might be greeted by a line that snakes back up the saddle! I've seen people waiting over 30 minutes just to get on the cables. Believe me, it is *much* easier to ascend the cables when you can go at your own pace.

Half Dome's cables await you

POI 9

Base of the cables
Elapsed Time......... 4 hours 30 minutes
Altitude.............. 8402 feet
Cumulative Distance.. 7.1 miles

Relax a bit at the base of the cables. Have a good drink and maybe a bite of an energy bar. You'll need all your reserves, so don't rush. Re-lace your boots. At the base of the cables, you may find several pairs of old gloves, discarded by those who went before you. They are trash, pure and simple; they are not put there as a public service. The Park Service discourages this type of littering—in fact, they'd appreciate your taking a few pairs down with you. Anyway, you'll be glad you have your bike gloves instead of the dirty, torn, rotted, and oversized garden gloves usually left there.

Collapse your poles and attach them securely to your fanny pack with Velcro straps. If you have faith in your fellow humans, you may try leaving your gear near a rock, but beware, the squirrels will gnaw at your pack to get to a snack. You'll notice that there is no ranger or authority to control who goes up. No age limits, no weight limits; just free passage to anyone willing. When you have your courage up, go for it! The cables are multi-stranded steel, about 1 inch in diameter, and have more than enough strength. They are attached to 3-foot stanchion poles and resemble a banister. The poles rest in holes drilled into the rock. Note that I said "rest." They will come out if you pull up on them. After this happens to you the first time, you'll forever treat them gingerly. At the base of every pole pair is a long two-inch-by-four-inch piece of wood placed perpendicular to the path. This allows you to stand every 10 feet and take a rest.

From the base to the top is a 425-foot vertical rise. The safest strategy here is to keep three points in contact at all times (hands and feet alternating between cables and rock). You'll get a better grip from your boots if you maintain a flat foot against the rock, rather than walking on your toes. Your leg muscles are large, and you'll fare better if they do most of the work. In the early days following the installation of the cable system, hikers clipped themselves to the cable with a rope around their waist. This clipping is still a good idea—only you can use modern carabiners to secure yourself. I do not recommend pulling out a camera for panorama shots while ascending. If you must take a picture, have the camera around your neck to minimize this insecure interval. If you are scared (who's not?), try not to look out. Focus on the 10 feet in front of you. Breathe deliberately, but don't hyper-ventilate. This is a difficult climb, but you can do it. About halfway up the rock, you'll encounter two discontinuities

Group ascending Half Dome in 1924 using clips tied to waist, then attached to each section of the cable

One step at a time

The slope up the cables is nearly 45 degrees

in its surface; this means you'll have to be prepared to step over these granite ledges. Be aware, also, that a couple of times the cable that you are clutching will descend back to the rock and end to be replaced by a new run of cable. (Each side of the cable system is actually several connected runs of cable anchored to the rock, not one continuous piece.) The transition of the cable as it drops down the rock can give you pause. You'll notice that the cable route is bi-directional. You'll have to lean out of the way so those coming down can pass. Be cautious of hikers with large backpacks. They may be unaware that their pack is swinging wide as they pass you. You don't need an unexpected bump to throw off your concentration.

Eventually, you'll see the rock slowly end its steep slope, and you'll be able to walk unaided but breathless. Depending on the traffic, this may have taken you 15 to 45 minutes. Congratulations. You did it!

Apex of Half Dome
Elapsed Time. . . . . 5 hours
Altitude. . . . . 8842 feet
Cumulative Distance. . 7.2 miles

Work your way to the very apex of the rock. Bask in your
accomplishment; high-five your mates. Use your cell phone (it
may work) to call your friends back home. Enjoy your lunch
and take a nap in the hot sun. Cautiously explore the rock.
There is not much up here. Half Dome is surprisingly large:
the surface approximates 17 football fields. The far western
end reveals a series of cairns or trail ducks (human-made
rock stacks) and little else. There are few trees left on the top
of Half Dome, most of which were cut for firewood decades
ago, when camping was allowed. Be cautious of loose gravel
on the surface. Be very aware of the edge and don't approach
it too closely, and do not throw anything over it, since climbers may be coming up the sheer vertical face. Be sure to get
your picture taken standing carefully on the Visor at the
northwest peak. It's an impressive shot, with nothing but air
under you. Gaze down on the valley—did you leave your car
lights on? The views are spectacular: The Yosemite Valley,
Glacier Point, El Capitan, Clouds Rest, Tenaya Canyon, the
Quarter Domes, Mt. Watkins, Mt. Hoffman, and others. Use
your park map to help locate these sights.

Watch for the marmots and squirrels. They are adept at
stealing a sandwich or munchies. Please don't feed them.
They need to forage for themselves, lest they starve once all
the tourists leave in the fall. (It amazes me how they get up
the rock in the first place!) Change into your dry socks. You
still have a long trek ahead. It is much easier going down the
cables. Spending one hour on the top is about right—any
longer and you'll really be stiff, and reluctant to begin the trip
back to camp.

The top of Half Dome is nearly devoid of vegetation

Friends gather on the top for lunch

The overhang resembles a visor

The cables down—take it slow!

View of Yosemite Valley, Glacier Point, and El Capitan

Now you start the long downhill trek. Good old gravity helps a lot. I suggest facing the rock as soon as it starts to get steep. Not only is facing out scarier, but you'll have little leverage with your wrists twisted. Again, the bike gloves will be appreciated as you feed the cable out during your descent. You'll have to say "excuse me" a lot as the late arrivers struggle up. The agony on their faces will make you appreciate your early start. Simply get a good grip, hold on to one of the cables, and lean out of the way to allow others to pass. On the way down, you can't help but gaze out at the spectacular view. If you are acrophobic, focus on the 10 feet in front of you. Should you feel any vertigo or a panic attack coming on, stop and breathe slowly. Inform your companions and slowly descend. You may try sitting down and sliding while holding on to the cables.

The Little Spring — again
Elapsed Time. . . . . 6 hours 45 minutes
Altitude. . . . . 7228 feet
Cumulative Distance. . 8.5 miles

You'll be seeing the same scenery on the way down that you saw on the way up, so I won't cover it again. This will be true until after Little Yosemite Valley when you take the Nevada Fall Trail instead of the Mist Trail back. Your knees will thank you. A comment about the trip down: it can be harder than the trip up. The stress on your knees will take its toll. Also, don't underestimate the length of the return. After a couple of hours, you'll think Curry Village is just around the next switchback—not so! Pace yourself and resist the temptation to run down (you'll see a few doing so). Running downhill is really, *really* bad for your knees. Keep drinking and moving.

Less than an hour after leaving the Dome, you'll once again see the Little Spring—now on the right side of the trail. You'll probably be carrying two drained water bottles by now. Fill them here; take a short rest, have a big drink, and keep going.

Little Yosemite Valley — again
Elapsed Time. . . . . 7 hours 45 minutes
Altitude. . . . . 6095 feet
Cumulative Distance. . 10.7 miles

After you complete the last of the switchbacks, you come out of the woods and settle into Little Yosemite Valley. The trail forks; go to the right. This is the most direct path. If nature calls, take the left fork, and you'll soon see the large, elevated wooden facility. You may see a trail sign pointing to the Backpackers Camp, which also leads to the toilets. This "mother of all johns" has four units available. These toilets don't get as much action as the others on the trail, so the odds are high that you'll find no lines. Okay, back on the trail. Catch another glimpse of the Merced to your left and continue.

Little Yosemite Valley toilets

Junction of Mist and John Muir Trails

POI 13

Elapsed Time. . . . . 8 hours 20 minutes
Altitude. . . . . 5950 feet
Cumulative Distance. . 11.7 miles

You're back now to the intersection of the two routes down (via Vernal Fall/Mist Trail or Nevada Fall/John Muir Trail). You'll see a gaggle of people converged here.

Decision time: the longer (maybe a half hour more) route via Nevada Fall or the shorter but steeper route via the Mist Trail? Unless you have a time-critical reason for going the Mist Trail, don't. Your knees will explode! There's really nothing to prove now. You already conquered Half Dome. Take the left trail. The sign at this point indicates 3.7 miles to the valley (the John Muir Trail). Head to Nevada Fall, just a few minutes' walk away. Look to your right and see Liberty Cap, then look down, and you'll see the trail leading to Vernal Fall.

POI 14	**Nevada Fall Bridge**
	Elapsed Time. . . . . 8 hours 30 minutes
	Altitude. . . . . 5977 feet
	Cumulative Distance. . 11.9 miles

This is a good spot to kick back and recharge. The area above the fall is usually packed with Half Dome veterans and others who did the day hike up from the valley. Take your shoes off and soak a bit. *Caution*: Do not go out into the placid-looking waters. There are deep holes and strong currents away from the shore. The rocks are slippery, and you can see what lies 50 yards downstream—Nevada Fall. It stands at 594 feet, and occasionally, somebody accidentally goes over. Treat some water and fill your water bottles, have an energy bar, and catch some rays. Give it 15 minutes and then get back on the trail. Before crossing the bridge, go down to the right side to an overlook (it's fenced), and gaze at the power of the water going over the edge. Continue across the bridge and keep on the John Muir Trail. The Panorama Trail will join from the left. This beautiful area features the Panorama Cliff. During the summer, it continually drips a refreshing stream of water, remnants of the snow pack. You can spot wildflowers growing out from the wall itself. The

The serene waters of the Merced above Nevada Fall

Close-up of Nevada Fall

The John Muir Trail at the Panorama Cliff

Final view of Half Dome with Liberty Cap in the foreground

Endless switchbacks on the trail home

sharp drop to your right provides an unobstructed view of
Nevada Fall, Liberty Cap, and Half Dome. Continue down,
and enjoy seemingly endless cycle of switchbacks.

Be alert for another trail sign. This one says, "Yosemite
Valley 2.3 miles"; keep on the John Muir Trail. At Clark
Point, don't take a spur that could take you back to the Mist
Trail. Continue for another 20 minutes, and you'll approach
another critical juncture. The sign advises: "Foot trail only.
Stock prohibited." This means if you diverge, you'll be on the
dusty mule trail. While this would indeed get you down to
the valley, this trail is not for hikers. Don't go left. If a pack-
animal party (horses or mules) approaches you, step aside
uphill, and remain quiet. Equestrians have the right of way.
Continue down the main trail; watch for trail signs to Vernal
Fall. When you can see the water of the Merced River, keep it
on your right and descend toward the bridge.

POI 15

Vernal Fall Bridge—again
Elapsed Time. . . . . 9 hours 53 minutes
Altitude. . . . . 4464 feet
Cumulative Distance. . 14.5 miles

Bring it home now. You've merged with the Mist Trail and are back to the bridge. The flush toilets will be on your left, and the water fountain will be on your right. Keep hydrating and get one last water refill. This area will be mobbed in the late afternoon, and you'll be glad you got all your pictures this morning.

POI 16

Mileage marker sign—again
Elapsed Time. . . . . 10 hours 30 minutes
Altitude. . . . . 4093 feet
Cumulative Distance. . 15.5 miles

After running the gauntlet of casual hikers, you reach the unofficial end of the adventure—the mileage marker sign and Happy Isles. By now, you should be too tired to care about taking more pictures. You'll be digging for that last energy bar to help you get back to camp. Take the same road out that you took in, and you should be back at Curry Village in another 15 minutes.

After the Hike

You've earned your wings—celebrate! I have a little ritual after my annual ascents. Once everyone in my party is back from the hike, I hold a ceremony for first timers. I have them all kneel in a circle and I "knight" each one with one of my hiking poles. I then present them with a Certificate of Accomplishment and pin on a Major Award—a Half Dome lapel pin. The ceremony is complete when they drink a swallow of beer from the sacred goblet of Ten-ie-ya (a paper cup).

After your quick celebration, head to the showers. They are located near the main complex of Curry Village; showers and towels are free for guests. If you aren't staying there, you can still use the showers for a small fee. Bring your own soap and shampoo, and plan to wait in line. Shower sandals are a good idea. Hot water is plentiful but the sheer numbers of humanity and the trail dust carried in can make the showers messy.

After your shower, you have several choices for dinner. The nearest ones are at the Curry Pavilion Buffet and the Pizza Deck and Curry Bar. If you want to see a different part of the valley, take the shuttle bus to the main Yosemite Village. You can dine at Degan's Loft or the Deli, or venture over to the Yosemite Lodge and enjoy its Mountain Room Restaurant. Dinner at The Ahwahnee is a real treat. Built in the 1920s this National Historic Landmark features historic architecture on a grand scale. The dining room is large, with a very tall ceiling with exposed beams. Be aware that the evening dress code here calls for jackets or sweaters—definitely no jeans or shorts. Some of the eateries close at 8 p.m.; some at 9 p.m. Check the times to make sure you don't miss dinner, and make reservations beforehand, if necessary. After dinner, good places to relive your adventures include The Ahwahnee Bar (open until 11 p.m.) or the Mountain Room Lounge (open until 10:30 p.m.). However, you'll probably be in bed well before then.

Rest assured that no matter how much you've prepared, you'll be sore tomorrow. Now buy that "I made it to the top" T-shirt!

I hope this book helps make your journey a bit easier.

See you on the trail.

Appendix:
Information Sources

Books

Bunnell, Lafayette H. *Discovery of the Yosemite and the Indian War of 1851 Which Led to That Event.* 4th ed. Yosemite Association, 1990.

Gillmore, Robert. *Great Walks: Yosemite National Park.* Great Walks, Inc., 1993.

Jones, William R. *Yosemite: The Story Behind the Scenery.* 2nd ed. KC Publishing, 1997.

Lanza, Michael. *Day Hiker's Handbook.* Seattle, WA: Mountaineers Books, 2003.

Madgic, Bob. *Shattered Air: A True Account of Catastrophe and Courage on Yosemite's Half Dome.* Springfield, NJ: Burford Books, 2005.

Saldana, Lori. *Lori Saldana's Backpacking Primer.* La Crescenta, CA: Mountain N'Air Books, 1995.

Schaffer, Jeffrey P. *Top Trails: Yosemite.* Berkeley, CA: Wilderness Press, 2007.

Schaffer, Jeffrey P. *Yosemite National Park: A Complete Hiker's Guide.* Wilderness Press, 2006.

Other Printed Matter

GPS Navigation Course Rev 1.3. Steve Wood/REI Outdoor School class handout. 2005.

"Half Dome." *Outside* Magazine, p. 94. June 2003.

Hiking Merit Badge pamphlet. Boy Scouts of America. 2004.

REI product information brochures (GPS, Trekking Poles, Hiking Boots, Water Filters). 2006.

Trails of Yosemite. Yosemite Association/NPS brochure. 1987.

Yosemite National Park and Vicinity. Topographic map. Berkeley CA: Wilderness Press, 2004.

Yosemite Association Quarterly Journal for Members. Fall 1998, Summer 2002, Winter 2003, Fall 2005, Summer 2006, Winter 2006.

Yosemite Today. Tabloid of park information, events, services. National Park Service and Delaware North Company. Monthly.

Websites

www.adventurebuddies.net—Benefits of and techniques for properly using trekking poles

www.firstgov.gov—U.S. Government portal for information about all agencies

www.HikeHalfDome.com — Author's site for information about the Half Dome hike

www.leki.com—World's leading manufacturer of trekking poles

www.katadyn.com—Water treatment products

www.nps.gov/yose—National Park Service site for Yosemite

www.nps.gov/archive/yose/planning/gmp/contents.html—General Management Plan, Visitor Use, Park Operations, and Development Plan for Yosemite National Park, 1980, Department of the Interior, National Park Service

www.nps.gov/archive/yose/planning/yvp—*Final Yosemite Valley Plan/ Supplemental Environmental Impact Statement (SEIS),* National Park Service, 2000

www.recreation.gov—Campsite reservations

www.recreation.gov/recpass.jsp —Federal Recreation Pass Programs

www.rei.com—Outdoor gear store and resource cooperative

www.sierraclub.org—Sierra Club home page

www.symg.com— Guided hikes and backpack trips in Yosemite and the Sierra Nevada

www.wunderground.com/US/CA/Yosemite_National_Park.html— Yosemite weather

www.yarts.com—Yosemite Area Regional Transportation System, info, schedules, tickets

www.yosemitefun.com—Commercial Yosemite information

www.yosemitegold.com—Commercial information for Yosemite and the Gold Country

www.yosemite.national-park.com—Commercial Yosemite National Park information page

www.yosemite.org—Yosemite Association

www.yosemitepark.com—Delaware North Company Parks & Resorts at Yosemite, Inc.

Phone Numbers

(209) 372-1407 Ahwahnee Lodge front desk

(801) 559-5000 Yosemite lodging reservations

(209) 372-1000 Main Yosemite business number

(800) 436-7275 NPS Campground reservations for domestic callers

(301) 722-1257 NPS Campground reservations for international callers

(209) 372-0322 Save-A-Bear hotline

(209) 379-2646 Yosemite Association

(209) 372-1274 Yosemite Lodge front desk

(209) 372-8344 Yosemite Mountaineering School

(209) 372-0200 Yosemite National Park information and road conditions

(209) 372-0740 Yosemite Valley Ranger Station

About the Author

Rick Deutsch lives in San Jose, California, with his wife. A veteran of Silicon Valley high tech, Rick is an adventure traveler. Some of his personal bests include rafting through the Grand Canyon (three times); ascending California's Mt. Whitney; hiking Mt. Shasta; twice pedaling the 500-mile Iowa RAGBRAI cross-state bike tour; mountain biking in Moab, Utah; scuba diving in Papua New Guinea, Palau, Truk Lagoon, the Caribbean, and the Galapagos; hiking Peru's Machu Picchu; and dogsledding in Alaska. It was after his 17th trek up Half Dome that he decided to write this guide to help others enjoy this fun and rewarding hike. Visit him at www.HikeHalfDome.com

Index

More Yosemite Titles from Wilderness Press

ISBN 0-89997-383-3

ISBN 978-0-89997-425-5

ISBN 0-89997-420-1

ISBN 0-89997-370-1

For ordering information, contact your local bookseller
or Wilderness Press, www.wildernesspress.com